Volume 2 Issue 1
2013

IMAGINATIO ET RATIO

A Journal of Theology and the Arts

This journal is available at www.wipfandstock.com/journals. A partial version in full color is available online at www.imaginatioetratio.org. For email subscriptions please visit www.imaginatioetratio.org.

Imaginatio et Ratio is published bi-annually by Wipf and Stock Publishers.
199 West 8th Avenue, Suite 3
Eugene, Oregon 97401, USA
ISBN: 978-1-62564-430-5

About

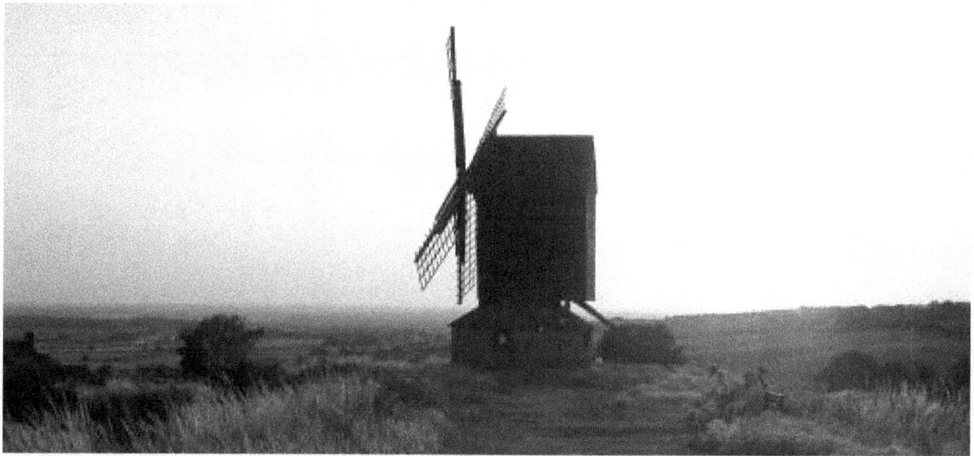

Imaginatio et Ratio is a peer reviewed journal primarily focusing on the intersection between the arts and theology, hoping to allow imagination and reason to be seen as intimately intertwined–as different expressions of the same divine truth. *Imaginatio et Ratio* was started in the hopes that it could serve a growing community of artists and thinkers and strives to present accessible but high quality art, literary fiction, creative non-fiction, and theology/philosophy–as well as interviews and book, film, art and music reviews. The journal is published twice a year and is available in print and a digital format.

Submission Guidelines

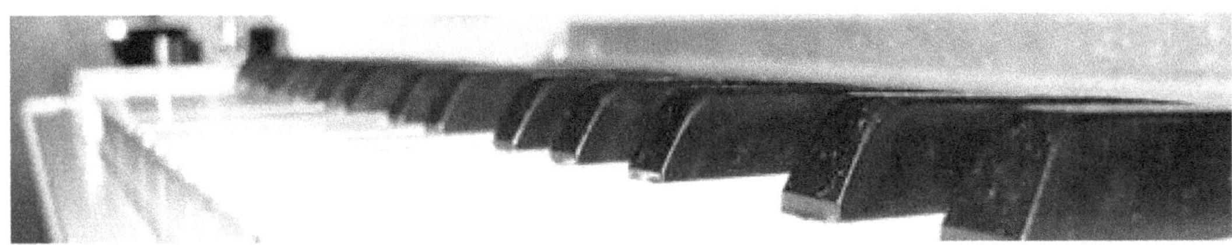

In general, we welcome the submission of essays, interviews, reviews (book, film, music, art), creative writing, and art that attempts to engage–implicitly or explicitly–Christian theology. The journal is published twice a year. Submissions are ongoing, so, depending on the time of submission, work will be considered for the appropriate issue.

Style and Format:

*Unsolicited submissions should be ready for blind peer review: no name on or in the attachment, just in the body of the email...

*Submissions should be accompanied by two separate documents: 1. a CV/Resume and 2. a brief bio (the brief bio will be included in the journal)...

*No previously published material...

*When appropriate, submissions should be sent in .doc format, 12 point Times New Roman font, no page numbers, single spaced...

*Total word count includes footnotes...

**Essays/Interviews:* Chicago Manual of Style (Footnotes), 1,000-6,000 words

**Reviews:* Chicago Manual of Style (Footnotes), 1,000-3,000 words

**Creative Writing:* Literary fiction and creative nonfiction, 1,000-6,000 words

**Art:* Submit art as JPEG images, with an explanatory paragraph describing the work (approximately 100-500 words)

**News/Events:* If you would like us to post your news/event/conference/etc. on the site, please send it along through the contact form at our website...

*Please allow up to ten weeks for decisions on submitted material...

*If your submission is accepted, a contract will be sent to you to sign and return: any other editing or formatting issues will be resolved at this time through e-mail. A proof will be sent to the author for her/his approval...

*Authors will retain the copyright of their work, while granting the journal right of first publication. Authors may use their contributions for other works as long as acknowledgement of the initial publication in this journal is noted...

*Unfortunately, the journal cannot offer compensation for published works...

*The editors make every effort to ensure accuracy, but the contributors are ultimately responsible for the accuracy of their work...

*The contributions in *Imaginatio et Ratio* do not necessarily reflect the views of the editors, the advisory board or Wipf and Stock Publishers...

*Send submissions to imaginatioetratio@gmail.com...

Acknowledgements

The cover photo was edited for this issue by Kevin C. Neece, incorporating artwork by Dawn Waters Baker (used with permission). "Magic, Muggles and Misunderstanding: A Conversation with Leigh Hickman About the Christ-like Wizard that Christian Culture Mistook for the Devil," by Kevin C. Neece, has been adapted here from work previously published with *New Identity* (http://issuu.com/newidentitymag/docs/issue13/37) and Art House Dallas (www.arthouseamerica.com/dallas-blog/harry-potter-pop-culture-and-the-affections-of-the-heart.html) Elijah Davidson's review of *Jurassic Park* 3D originally appeared on Reel Spirituality (http://www.brehmcenter.com/initiatives/reelspirituality/film/reviews/jurassic-park) and is reprinted here with permission from Reel Spirituality and the author.

Table of Contents

Volume 2 Issue 1
2013

Editorial, *Imaginatio et Ratio: A Journal of Theology and the Arts*, Volume 2, Issue 1: "Other Worlds: Sci-Fi/Fantasy 2013"

Kevin C. Neece

I'm grateful to my friend and colleague, Senior Editor Jeff Sellars, for allowing me the honor of welcoming you to this, the inaugural Sci-Fi/Fantasy issue of *Imaginatio et Ratio*. This is our first themed issue and we're looking forward to more in the future. The idea for this project arose both from our love of science fiction and fantasy and from the pool of very talented potential contributors we were discovering and were already associated with in this genre. In these pages are colleagues and friends—old and new—who are particularly skilled at bringing us into, as this issue's title suggests, "Other Worlds."

Of course, while an academic publication is generally thought of as concerning the rational—documentation, critical analysis and formality—our journal's very title implies a broadening of that perspective. "Imaginatio et Ratio," or "Imagination and Reason," is both our moniker and our guiding principle. To us, free and creative thought and expression need not be divorced from careful analysis and academic rigor. In fact, we see the two as not only existing comfortably side-by-side, but also necessarily and intrinsically informing one another. Our pursuit of knowledge and understanding extends to every area of human expression and experience, especially with reference to our essential connection to the Author of the universe. It is perhaps through our creative and artistic endeavors that we most often, and most uniquely, express that we are indeed created in his image. As the human story encompasses both the plainly knowable and the mysteriously oblique, so also does God make himself known and simultaneously keep himself hidden. In our "reaching for the invisible God," as Philip Yancey puts it, we are seeking a relationship wherein we know and are known by the Greatest Unknown.

It is therefore essential that our theology encompass a great wideness of mystery, at home with the ineffable, in conversation with the imperceptible, and ever-present, even on the outer edges of our reality. Reason and mystery must coexist. This kind of symbiosis between the speculative and the scientific, the dreamlike and the definite, is perhaps at the core of the narrative and thematic underpinnings of both science fiction and fantasy. These two genres, in many ways disparate (technology vs. magic, action/adventure vs. quest narrative, etc.), are nonetheless uniquely intertwined, as they both set about the business of building worlds within which to tell stories both fantastic and realistic in a quest to explore the human condition, the pursuit of virtue and an encounter with the unknown. Whether aliens in outer space, sprites and faeries in a dark forest or speculative technology that may as well be magic, the stories in science fiction and fantasy deal in often wildly imagined places and people that take us outside the familiar, to realms in which we may seek new understanding and an expanded vision of our own reality—should we indeed decide to return there.

Appropriately, it seems the pages following this one raise more questions than they provide answers. As two dragons peer out at us—perhaps hungrily, perhaps angrily—do they seek to devour us? Are they sulking against defeat and imprisonment? Or are we looking into a mirror? When we find ourselves scuttled away to a place buried in a magical, subterranean envelope of space-time, where temptations abound and the means of survival go stubbornly against instinct, how will we hold our own against potentially deadly enchantments?

In this issue, we'll imagine a future that could only be constructed in the 19th Century and run headlong into adventure, mystery and the juxtaposition of emotional fragility with the dogged denial of a soft and beating heart. An intelligent ape will share his thoughts on faith, reason and the nature of humankind. How will we respond if some of his words ring true? Do cybernetic zombies seek to devour our souls instead of our flesh? And is there light to be found in the much-loved and oft-maligned story of a wizard who just might work the magic of redemption? This and more will be explored as we journey from the corridors of a wandering space vessel to the city streets of a new human colony with our fingers between the pages of books on philosophy and theology.

Amidst these essays, stories, paintings and poems, we hope that you will find questions to explore, unexplained voyages to embark upon and a Light to guide you along the way. As we engage in the uniquely human practice of imagination and wonder, perhaps we will catch glimmers—like starlight and faerie wings—of what it means to live as the creative image-bearers of the Inventor of creativity itself. So pull out your wand, strap on your goggles and engage your warp drive. Other worlds await us.

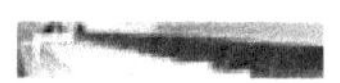

Essays

Zombie Trek: Humanity, Fear and a Fate Worse Than Death in Star Trek's Borg Narratives – Part One

Kevin C. Neece

The Borg are one of Star Trek's most popular—and arguably most frightening—villains. At first, they almost seem too dark for the franchise, which is often popularly thought of as clean, shiny and almost sterile. If one looks deeper, however, one finds that darkness has always been at the edges of Star Trek, even if its world may at times seem too perfect. Perhaps that has something to do with what makes the Borg such an excellent foil for our Starfleet heroes—they give form to darkness and fears that live on the edges of the Star Trek universe. Pale, unthinking, shuffling forward in herds and assimilating others to become like themselves, the Borg also resemble perhaps the most prevalent craze of our current pop culture epoch: zombies. Could this parallel shed light on why the Borg work so well in Star Trek? Perhaps. First, however, it seems prudent to ask: Do the Borg truly qualify as zombies?

Objections may be made to this parallel over dissimilarities between the Borg and zombies. The Borg are not dead, they do not eat flesh and they share a hive mind, or collective consciousness. By contrast, zombies must die to be zombified, are driven by hunger for living tissue (especially brains, in many versions) and are basically mindless. These objections are valid; however, they are limited in their scope, both in terms of the history and varieties of the zombie archetype itself and the most important reasons for drawing the parallel in the first place. These noted dissimilarities are between the Borg and a single type of zombie—the flesh-devouring undead depicted in such widely popular recent films and television as *28 Days Later*, the *Resident Evil* video game and film series, this summer's *World War Z* and *The Walking Dead*, currently the most-watched show on television. But this "horror zombie" is only the most recent form of zombie to arise.

In fact, the zombie archetype is very old and has existed in at least three major forms. The horror zombie is a very recent invention, beginning with George A. Romero's 1968 film, *Night of the Living Dead*. Though the film itself never actually uses the word "zombie," instead referring to its undead as "ghouls," the basic horror zombie archetype established here laid the groundwork for everything in the genre that has followed. Romero himself later embraced the term "zombie" and set the standard for the modern zombie film with his sequel to *Living Dead*, the 1978 film *Dawn of the Dead*. In that film, the now familiar zombie horde, complete with rotting flesh, open wounds and torn clothing, stalks the local shopping mall in an orgy of appetite that rather obviously seeks to comment on American consumerism.

Today's horror zombies are indeed frequently referred to Romero zombies, but that moniker, if too broadly applied, misses some of the breadth and history of the horror zombie motif. Other filmmakers such as Dan O'Bannon (whose *Return of the Living Dead*, based on John A. Russo's 1978 novel, spawned several sequels) have placed their own unique stamp on Romero's zombies. Conversely, Romero's films were influenced by such previous works as EC Comics' 1950s series *Tales From the Crypt*. Undead attackers are also traced back as far as the *Epic of Gilgamesh*[1] and some have even claimed that zombies appear in the Bible.[2] Of course,

[1] Specifically, the referenced occurs in these lines from the goddess Ishtar in Tablet VI: "I will knock down the Gates of

these "Biblical zombies" are more examples of modern readers drawing creative parallels with zombies and often grossly misrepresent the Biblical text. Their existence does serve, however, to expose the prevalence of zombies in the modern imagination. This Biblical category could also include the very poor characterization of the resurrected Jesus or Lazarus as zombies. As will be seen in the two older zombie archetypes, however, it takes a great deal more than returning from the dead to qualify one as a zombie. In fact, returning from the dead is not always necessary.

Of the two remaining zombie archetypes, it is difficult to say which is older. However, the classic zombie until recent decades has been what could be called the "Voodoo zombie." In West African and Haitian forms of Voodoo, a bokor, or sorcerer, has the power to resurrect and control a person's dead body. This *zombi* (as the term was originally rendered) is then totally under the control of the bokor. A similar belief exists in South Africa that witches may possess the dead in order to use them as slaves.[3]

This archetype entered western pop culture in a variety of forms, most notably in classic horror films like *White Zombie* (1932) and *I Walked With a Zombie* (1943). The Voodoo zombie differs a great deal from the horror zombie in that it does not feed on flesh. It is kept alive, instead, by magical means. Additionally, the Voodoo zombie is a slave, under the direct control of the bokor, rather than roaming aimlessly or within a horde of other zombies. Where horror zombies seem to head in the same direction because they are all chasing the same meal, Voodoo zombies do only the bidding of their master.

It should be noted that, though this form of zombie has certainly had a place in pop culture, it is based on a belief in something that, for practitioners of Voodoo (or Vodou), is very real. Though many attempts have been made to investigate stories of "real zombies," particularly in Haiti, no evidence has been found to conclusively give credence to the existence of true Voodoo zombies. The trouble, of course, has been finding an explanation for how a bokor could both appear to resurrect an individual and make that person a zombie. While some drugs exist that will induce a death-like state and others, like scopolamine and other so-called "zombie drugs" can put people into states of extreme suggestibility,[4] the effects are short-lived and so, often, are the victims themselves. In Voodoo beliefs, when one becomes a zombie, one remains under the control of the bokor forever.[5]

It is this aspect of control and a master/slave relationship, often alongside a similarly mystical or magical power, that qualifies the next zombie archetype as a zombie. As we have seen, the image of the reanimated dead dates back to some of the earliest written texts, but perhaps equally ancient is the idea of the trance state and enchantment by a sorcerer or other person or being with special powers. For example, the Greek mythological figure of the siren is

---

the Netherworld, I will smash the door posts, and leave the doors flat down, and will let the dead go up to eat the living! And the dead will outnumber the living!" Retrieved from http://www.ancienttexts.org/library/mesopotamian/gilgamesh/tab6.htm

2 Zechariah 14:12, Isaiah 66:24, and Ezekiel 37:10

3 Niehaus, Isak (June 2005). "Witches and Zombies of the South African Lowveld: Discourse, Accusations and Subjective Reality". *The Journal of the Royal Anthropological Institute* 11(2): 197–198.

4 Otis, John, "Columbia: Beware the Zombie Drug," *Global Post*, June 17, 2013, Accessed June 20, 2013, http://www.globalpost.com/dispatch/news/regions/americas/colombia/130614/colombia-scopolamine-drug.

5 For further information, see: Mars, Louis P. (1945). "The Story of Zombi in Haiti". *Man* 45(22): 38–40. doi:10.2307/2792947. JSTOR 2792947; Booth, W. (1988), "Voodoo Science", *Science*, 240: 274–277; Hines, Terence; "Zombies and Tetrodotoxin"; *Skeptical Inquirer*; May/June 2008; Volume 32, Issue 3; Pages 60–62; Wilentz, Amy, "A Zombie Is a Slave Forever," Haiti: NYTimes.com, October 26, 2012, Accessed June 20, 2013, http://www.nytimes.com/2012/10/31/opinion/a-zombie-is-a-slave-forever.html?_r=0

an enchantress who lures sailors from the sea with a song so beautiful that they are content to sit and listen to it until they die and their bodies rot.[6]

Here, however, we are interested in the enchanted, entranced or spellbound person who is the mindless slave of another—what might be termed the "hypno zombie" or "mind control zombie." Though the enchanted slave is an ancient concept, its entry into the modern popular imagination probably begins with the hypnotist. Since the 19th Century, the image of the hypnotist and his subject has been a strong popular image of enchantment and magical power. The popular idea of hypnotism is that the person in trance is totally under the control of the hypnotist, obeying his or her every command without question. Of course, this trope has little to do with real clinical hypnosis, but taps into a very old idea of bewitching and beguiling another to do one's bidding. In science fiction, this often takes the form of mind control, a similar process carried out by any number of gadgets, headgear and rays that, through various means, suppress the will of a victim and place them under the control of the person wielding the technology. In whatever form it appears, this hypno zombie shares with the Voodoo zombie the characteristics of being a blank slate, essentially a mindless puppet, obedient only to its master. The hypno zombie is prevalent across media and literature, from Greek mythology to Saturday morning cartoons.

The hypno zombie differs from both the horror zombie and the Voodoo zombie in at least one significant way: this is a zombie who has not died. This makes the zombie condition less permanent.[7] In fact, it is almost always reversed when the hero triumphs over the villain. The zombie horde quality of the horror zombie also appears frequently with hypno zombies, as villains use music, sound waves, gas or some other such device to entrance large numbers of victims at once. These zombies usually move as a horde, but do so under the control of their master.

Historically, then, the word "zombie" has been used to describe more than just a Romero or horror zombie. In fact, since the word "zombie" actually originates as the word *zombi* from Voodoo (or Vodou) beliefs, it could be said that the Voodoo zombie is perhaps the only true zombie. The other two zombie archetypes are zombies because the term has been, generally retroactively, applied to them. They are so named because of similarities they share with the Voodoo zombie. Specifically, the horror zombie earns the name by virtue of being a reanimated corpse, while the hypno zombie qualifies because it is a mindless slave. Most properly, then, the classification of a fictional creature as a zombie has to do, not with its similarity or dissimilarity to the horror zombie, but with whether it shares sufficient characteristics in common with the Voodoo zombie to be similarly grandfathered into the terminology.

In the second part of this paper, I will establish how the Borg relate to the zombie mythos by combining elements of all three historic zombie archetypes. I will also address anomalies in the Borg zombie, such as the collective consciousness and the technological aspects of Borg zombification. Then, I will explore how the Borg serve as a particular threat for the Star Trek universe, highlighting both the fundamental philosophical and spiritual threat they pose and how they address the same human fears as the overall zombie mythos within the Star Trek universe.

---

[6] Homer, *The Odyssey*

[7] To be fair, many cinematic portrayals of Voodoo zombies do not include the idea that the zombified person was a reanimated corpse. These, however, are not true Voodoo zombies, but hypno zombies with Voodoo zombie trappings. Similarly, the Voodoo zombie is augmented somewhat in a film like *White Zombie*, where a zombie is revealed to have only appeared to die. This similarly allows the zombie to be de-zombified. A zombie from real Voodoo beliefs, however, is a reanimated dead person.

Part Two of "Zombie Trek: Humanity, Fear and a Fate Worse Than Death in Star Trek's Borg Narratives" will appear in the next issue of this journal.

Violent Monotheists, Violent Corporations, and the Body: *Caprica*'s Theological Vision

Jake Andrews

In *De doctrina christiana* 2.6.7, Augustine emphasizes that images – by nature – are more delightful than the simple repetition of theological concepts. He describes the church and baptism in propositional terms before he quotes Song of Songs 4.2: 'Your teeth are like a flock of shorn sheep ascending from the pool, all of which give birth to twins and there is not a barren one among them.' Augustine suggests that this image communicates the theological concept in a more delightful way than if one were simply to describe it: 'Does a person learn anything different from when he hears it in plain words without the aid of this image? And nevertheless – I do not know why – I consider the saints more pleasant [*suavius*] when I picture them as the teeth of the church cutting people off from errors and transferring them to its body, softening hardness, as biting off and chewing.' In what follows, I want to leave aside that Augustine speaks here specifically about scripture's ability to delight, and to consider the general assertion that sometimes it is better to learn from reflecting on an image than from hearing an explanation, to allow ourselves to feel delight in contemplation of a pictorial representation. The image can help us think through ideas which have been discussed again and again in theological texts and can thereby persuade us of their truthfulness. Perhaps slightly more provocatively, I aim to demonstrate that a television show like *Caprica* has such power.

To move from speaking of a single image to a television show, it would be helpful to supplement Augustine's appeal to delight with Maurice Merleau-Ponty's description of film as 'a temporal *gestalt*.'[1] That is, a film – and on Merleau-Ponty's terms we can include a television show – is more than the sum of its parts; it is a cohesive whole that develops through time.[2] 'A film', Merleau-Ponty suggests, 'does not mean anything but itself', and by that, he means that the work of art begins with an idea, which 'is presented in a nascent state and emerges from the temporal structure of the film.' Its function 'is not to make these facts or ideas known to us',[3] but simply to be itself, a temporalized object with its own 'overall cinematographical rhythm', which 'leaves in the memory not a set of ideas but rather the emblem and the monogram of those ideas.'[4] While it might be possible to express the plot of a film, or even its thematic point, in a sentence or two, the artwork cannot be reduced to that expression precisely because the film is itself a temporalized object we perceive: 'The meaning of a film is incorporated into its rhythm just as the meaning of a gesture may immediately be read in that gesture.'[5] For that reason, Merleau-Ponty insists that film (and thereby television) 're-educates' us in how we see the world.[6]

---

1 Maurice Merleau-Ponty, 'The Film and the New Psychology', in *Sense and Non-Sense*, trans. Hubert Dreyfus and Patricia Allen Dreyfus (Evanston, Ill.: Northwestern University Press, 1964), 48-59 (54). I am indebted to Christina Chandler Andrews for comments on this essay, for several personal discussions concerning Merleau-Ponty's philosophy, and for providing access to her PhD thesis ('The Transfiguring Event: Phenomenological Readings of Ian McEwan's Late Fiction', [PhD diss., University of St Andrews, 2011]), which details Merleau-Ponty's ideas on art.

2 For more on this concept, see Eric Matthews, *The Philosophy of Merleau-Ponty* (Cheshem, Acumen: 2002), 141-143.

3 Merleau-Ponty, 'The Film and the New Psychology', 57. Eric Matthews, *Merleau-Ponty: A Guide for the Perplexed* (London: Continuum, 2006), 149, says: 'to look at the world afresh [. . .] is precisely what, according to Merleau-Ponty, modern art, literature, music and film enable us to do.'

4 Maurice Merleau-Ponty, *The World of Perception*, trans. Oliver Davis (London: Routledge, 2004), 73, 76. 'Cinematographical rhythm' refers to the overall combination of scenes, selected camera shots, music, dialogue, etc.

5 Merleau-Ponty, 'The Film and the New Psychology', 57.

6 Merleau-Ponty, 'The Film and the New Psychology', 53-54.

These two concepts – the persuasive delightfulness of an image and the temporality of cinema – provide a way into reflection on the television show *Caprica*. I suggest that by forcing the viewer to watch embodiments of certain concepts extended through time, the television show might well prove more persuasive than simply stating the concepts in propositional terms. At least two important theological concepts come to the surface when one pauses and reflects on *Caprica*. First, by removing all trace of any non-religious sphere, the show imagines a world that echoes John Milbank's argument that secular society is founded on an 'ontology of violence', and that it is in fact not neutral but in a very real sense, 'neo-pagan'.[7] Second, by showing the effects of disembodied existence in a cyber-world, and by showing the inhumanity of such existence, *Caprica* prompts reflection upon Christian theology's emphasis on incarnate, embodied existence and the resurrection of the body. While Milbank and others helpfully – and necessarily – point out these realities in their theological texts, I want to suggest that, like Augustine's propositional description of the church and baptism, such accounts can usefully be supplemented by reflection on a television program like *Caprica*, which can *show* these concepts to the viewer precisely by being a temporal *gestalt* and embodying a certain world. In the process of watching and meditating on it, the viewer may be delighted and persuaded into perceiving the world as it really is.

At the start, however, perhaps a disclaimer is required. An academic, propositional argument that highlights the more persuasive nature of temporal narrative and of images may seem ironic or even self-contradictory.[8] For that reason, the following pages take a cue from Merleau-Ponty's methodology and allow the academic, theological argument to arise out of discussion of the narrative arc of *Caprica*.[9] In the section on violence, the article emphasizes *Caprica* as temporal *gestalt* by drawing the theological point out of a discussion of the plot's gradual development, while the section on embodiment highlights the show's use of persuasive images.[10]

1. A Brief Orientation to *Caprica*

Caprica is a spin-off of the popular and critically-acclaimed *Battlestar Galactica* reboot and aired in 2010-11. Set after a suicide bomber destroys a 'Mag-Lev train', it is a reflection of the post-9/11 world. There are, of course, other themes – it engages, for instance, with how a parent grieves for his or her child, or how the media affects our view of the world – but they all take place within a world marred by terrorist attacks.

Roughly speaking, *Caprica* follows three groups of people. First, there are the polytheistic Capricans, represented mainly by Daniel and Amanda Graystone, parents of Zoe Graystone. The Global Defense Department (GDD) thinks Zoe is the suicide bomber responsible for destroying the train because she is a member of the 'Soldiers of the One' (STO), a

[7] John Milbank, *Theology and Social Theory: Beyond Secular Reason*, 2nd ed. (London: Blackwells, 2006), 278-326; 3. For a helpful primer on Milbank and Radical Orthodoxy, see: James K. A. Smith, *Introducing Radical Orthodoxy: Mapping a Post-Secular Theology* (Baker 2004).

[8] When presenting the initial draft of this article to the *Institute for Theology, Imagination, and the Arts* seminar at the University of St Andrews, I used clips from the television show. Here, narrative necessarily replaces these. I am grateful for the comments I received at the ITIA seminar as well as for further comments from Gavin Hopps.

[9] Merleau-Ponty, 'Metaphysics and the Novel', in *Sense and Nonsense*, 26-40; in this essay, Merleau-Ponty's argument arises from a close engagement with Simone de Beauvoir's *L'Invitée* (*She Came to Stay*). To use the terminology of Richard Viladesau (*Theology and the Arts: Encountering God through Music, Art and Rhetoric* [New York: Paulist, 2000], 124-164), I see *Caprica* as a 'text *for* theology', in the sense that it shows the human situation, but precisely in the theological reflection on it, *Caprica* can be seen as a 'text *of* theology' because it – though unconsciously – meditates on the very realities theologians like Milbank discuss.

[10] Both aspects are crucial to understanding the television show as artwork, and though this article artificially – and incompletely – separates them, *Caprica*'s persuasiveness arises precisely from their union.

monotheistic group known for their terrorist cells. The STO represents the second group, headed by Sister Clarice Willow. They are a monotheistic group from the planet Gemenon, who advocate 'the worship of a single, all-knowing, all-powerful god' ('Pilot'). The third plot strand follows Taurons who live on Caprica, represented primarily by Joseph Adama and his brother Sam. Joseph loses his wife and daughter in the Mag-Lev bombing, and he and his brother work for a crime syndicate called the Ha'la'tha.

The opening scene of *Caprica* throws the viewer immediately into the midst of a rave, while the camera pans and turns and tilts, showing the viewer a room teeming with teenagers dancing with abandon. Before the viewer can orientate him- or herself, the scene cuts to another room, more darkly lit, with red hues, filled with people in all manners of sexual activities. Once again, the viewer is back in the large room, but only for a second before the scene cuts to two men punching each other, blood splattering the crowd, who watch on cheering. The scene cuts to the large room, and it again cuts quickly, this time, to a man being shot multiple times, his murderer cheered on by the crowd. The camera pans up to the darkness, and for the first time, we catch a glimpse of Zoe Graystone, looking down – literally and metaphorically – on the debauchery. She makes eye contact with what, we will soon find out, is a digital version of herself, an avatar. The music shifts; the light goes red, and we see a man holding a large knife in front of the audience. After a woman dances on the stage, the audience drags up a screaming young woman. It is a ritual sacrifice. As the audience chants, 'kill, kill, kill', Zoe, her avatar, and her friends look on as the man lifts the knife and kills the woman. Once more, the scene cuts, but this time to Zoe sitting in a bathroom stall at school before a schoolmate interrupts; over Zoe's face is a 'holoband'. The world to which we have just been introduced is virtual, an immersive but nonetheless unreal place: 'V-World'. Outside the school and in the 'real' world, Zoe meets with her friends, Ben and Lacy, and they talk before finishing with a credal statement: 'For the one true god knows all and directs us all. So say we all.'

This opening scene introduces us both to the idea of a virtual world, where there appear to be no rules, and to the monotheistic teenagers, one of whom will carry out the suicide bombing that sets the tone for the rest of the series. Such a juxtaposition forces the viewer to grapple immediately with two concepts that structure *Caprica*. First, there is the virtual world, where the lack of bodily consequences allows people to exert their will-to-power in violent acts they would never commit in the 'real' world. And second, a link is established between the suicide bomber, Ben, who believes he will be rewarded in the afterlife for an act of violence in the 'real' Caprica City, and the violent tendencies of all the people in the disembodied world. Such a link plays a vital role in the show's depiction of the afterlife as either embodied or disembodied.

Later in *Caprica*, we are introduced to another place in V-World, 'New Cap City', a fully realized digital replica of the 'real-world' Caprica City, a game environment where there is only one rule: as in 'real' life, when you die, you can never come back. In 'The Imperfections of Memory', Joseph is introduced to New Cap City, and he can't figure out why someone would invent a world that is just like the 'real' world, to which his guide says, 'It's the kind of world where you can shoot someone in the head without going to jail, frak fifty women in one night without taking vinegra, how 'bout that?' Again, the theme from the opening scene appears: in a world with no 'real' consequences, people will exert their will-to-power in more and more violent ways.

In parallel with this theme, *Caprica* follows the inventor and corporate magnate Daniel Graystone as he attempts to create a genuine artificial intelligence. As the first minutes of the series demonstrate, however, his daughter has beaten him to it. He spends the majority of the show trying to use Zoe's avatar to re-create the program. His primary goal is to create a defense robot for the government (the Cylons of *Battlestar Galactica*), but he sees a more lucrative possibility: perpetual life. Daniel has lost his daughter in the Mag-Lev bombing and searches for any way to get her back. And while he seeks to recreate Zoe's program by stealing a Meta-Cognitive Processor (MCP) from his business rival, Thomas Vergis, Zoe's contact with the STO, Sister Clarice, wants the program as well. The STO want it to develop a virtual heaven. As we will see below, Daniel's idea of eternal life is one of embodiment, while Clarice's version is disembodied, 'virtual'.

To summarize: the show interweaves several plotlines, all of which engage the realities of a post-9/11, internet-saturated world. The show meditates on technology, religion, and death, and in what follows, I want to focus on two interlocking themes. The first is the binary initially posited between the tolerant, capitalistic polytheists and the violent monotheists. The second is the show's ideas about resurrection and apotheosis.

2. Violent Monotheists, Violent Corporations: *Caprica* as Temporal *Gestalt*

It is certainly a commonplace now to suppose that appeal to a single, all-powerful god leads inevitably to arrogance and, ultimately, to violence in that god's name.[11] The secular is a neutral arbiter of rationality and truth – so the argument goes – and it is the only real hope for peace. Of course, such an easy narrative has been drawn into question. For example, as John Milbank says, 'Once, there was no secular'.[12] And indeed, he goes on to say, we might even now conclude that there is no such thing, that the real binary that exists is in fact the sacred and the profane, or the 'neo-pagan'.[13] Underlying this 'Anti-Christianity' is an 'ontology of difference' with a 'presupposition of transcendental violence', an ontology whose ethical terminus is, ultimately, fascism.[14] For Milbank, then, there is no neutral realm of the secular from which a humanist morality can necessarily be derived.[15] Instead, the secular is itself religious (or anti-religious), a reestablishment of the pagan *mythos*, though re-formed in conscious reaction to the Christian *mythos*.[16] So, while it is often considered self-evident that monotheism tends towards violence, Milbank argues that there is, in fact, an underlying violence built into the very presuppositions of the secular project. There is no neutral, religionless realm; even the most peaceful-appearing consumerism harbors beneath its surface a nihilistic violence.

Caprica is a temporal *gestalt* that invites reflection and opens up the possibility of perceiving something that theologians like Milbank say. It questions the premise so often taken for granted in contemporary thought: that the capitalistic society, the one privileging diversity, freedom, and democracy, is capable of bringing peace, while explicitly religious viewpoints inevitably lead to conflict. The show removes the neutral realm of the secular by making the Capricans religious: they are polytheists. Still, when first introduced to the monotheists – or

---

[11] Leaving aside less-nuanced proponents, one might mention Regina M. Schwartz, *The Curse of Cain: The Violent Legacy of Monotheism* (Chicago: Chicago University Press, 1997).

[12] Milbank, *Theology and Social Theory*, 9. For another example, see: David Bentley Hart, *Atheist Delusions: The Christian Revolution and Its Fashionable Enemies* (New Haven: Yale University Press, 2009).

[13] Milbank, *Theology and Social Theory*, 3. Milbank is clear that 'neo-pagan' is not the best term for the 'secular' because the secular is actually 'a refusal of Christianity' that invents an 'Anti-Christianity' (280).

[14] Milbank, *Theology and Social Theory*, 297. For Milbank's alternative, positive ethical system, 'Socialism by grace', see id., *Being Reconciled: Ontology and Pardon* (London: Routledge, 2003), esp. 162-186.

[15] As Hart states, 'the highest ideals animating the secular project are borrowed ideals' (*Atheist Delusions*, 238).

[16] For a similar perspective, but with comment on the modern notion of freedom, see also: David Bentley Hart, *The Beauty of the Infinite: The Aesthetics of Christian Truth* (Grand Rapids: Eerdmans, 2003), esp. 431-439.

'monads' – they are portrayed as a violent, fringe sect that disturbs the peace of the pluralistic society. Daniel Graystone, in contrast, represents the polite, polytheistic, peaceful Capricans. He has made his way from poverty to wealth by the creation of the holoband, and he lives in a white, well-lit house with large windows looking out on a serene lake. The show establishes this binary early on, lulling the viewer into a mostly familiar world with its violent, religious fanatics, and its peaceful, white businessmen. The opposition remains relatively stable for five episodes, forcing the viewer to experience its breakdown gradually, through time, in a way that supplements an argument like Milbank's. Indeed, such temporality might prove more persuasive than only making the argument in propositional terms.

In the sixth episode of the show, 'Know Thy Enemy', *Caprica* brings the two sides together, beginning to demonstrate their proximity and overlap. The episode begins peaceably enough at a business reception. As Daniel and Amanda dance in the natural light streaming through the windows, laughing, he looks back, into a gloomy side room, and sees Tomas Vergis, his rival. They have a polite, though obviously acidic, discussion before Vergis reveals that he knows Daniel stole his computer chip, and that Daniel also killed two of his employees. Though Daniel is, until this point, unaware of the murders, he reacts calmly and denies the allegation. Throughout the discussion – one can note in viewing just how polite it is, how civilized – they stand beside a large statue of a bird-of-prey standing over its victims, a token of the violent undercurrents of their discussion, a hint of the violence yet to come.

Later, we see the Graystone corporate building before the scene cuts to Vergis and Daniel having lunch. Again, the civility of the scene is foregrounded; one can note the polite banter, the stark, clean room, the laughter, the sharing of a meal. This is the surface of the corporate enterprise: peaceful, cooperative, but with a seedy undertone. The viewer knows Daniel stole the chip, and Daniel himself has begun to believe people might have been murdered in the process. This is the underside of business. In 'Know Thy Enemy', it begins to become obvious that the capitalist enterprise arises from bloodshed, a fact masked by the hygienic beauty of the buildings, the business suits, and the choreographed civility of their exchanges, but one nonetheless always present. Even later in the episode when Vergis says, 'We are friendly competitors; we are not deadly rivals', the words are a mask for something deeper and more threatening. When he finally confronts Daniel in his own home, he says, 'You stole from me. I forgive that; that's good business. But the two deaths that you are responsible for – those men were like brothers to me.' Even Vergis tries to tease apart the deaths from the theft, but – as it unfolds over the course of hours – *Caprica* depicts something different; the show embodies the world of corporate business and allows the viewer to perceive its inherent violence, which corporations attempt to cover over with polite conversations in immaculate buildings.

This episode introduces the STO terrorist Barnabas Greely. When first seen, he is wrapping barbed wire around his arm, drawing blood because, as he says, 'Pain keeps our brain from going down bad paths.' He and his companions are located in an abandoned warehouse, not in a clean, well-lit building, and the violence is right on the surface. It is, as it were, more visible with these monotheistic terrorists. They are a reality the viewers of the show will find convincing, playing as it does in a post-9/11 world. But throughout the show's run, it becomes evident that the very ones critiquing the terrorists – polytheistic, tolerant, capitalists – are simply cloaking their own violence.

The violence of the corporate enterprise comes closer to the surface in episode eleven, 'Retribution', where there is another close juxtaposition between the STO and Daniel. Having lost his company to Vergis, Daniel allies with the Ha'la'tha to get it back. Their chosen method is blackmail, what one might classify as a 'white collar' crime, one that, in other words, involves no real violence.[17] In one scene, however, while Daniel threatens to blackmail a board member, Cornell, the violence simmers just below the surface. Cornell is ripped from his home by the Ha'la'tha, dragged and pushed into Daniel's presence. In the end, he kills himself, the blood splatter on the window of his car – vivid onscreen – a mark of the violence perpetuated in the pursuit of corporate business. The violence has surfaced, but still Daniel, the corporation's figurehead, has not directly committed violence himself. Later, Cornell's wife blames Daniel for her husband's death – 'What kind of man are you? You're a murderer.' – but Daniel is sealed off, protected in the confines of his corporate car. He can drive away from her, but the viewer knows he is guilty, that though he did not pull the trigger himself, he is a murderer. The violence is, once more, not quite out in the open, but it is certainly present.

In the same episode, Barnabas attempts to blow up a spaceport, while Clarice murders several who betrayed her. Finally, she and Barnabas come face-to-face, but not before Barnabas shoots his operative, Keon. This point is important, as the episode involves numerous deaths, but only two by gunshot: Cornell's and Keon's. The monotheists are more noticeably violent – they do, after all pull the trigger themselves – but the violent undercurrents of Daniel's corporate machinations are beginning to surface. The point is made visually: both the corporate machinations of blackmail and the plots of the monotheistic terrorists end in exactly the same place: blood and death. Here at least, the violence perpetuated by Daniel's corporation sits in the background – a man killing himself in a car – while the murdering rampage of the monads makes their own complicity in violence evident.

However, in the next episode, 'Things We Lock Away', Daniel's transition is complete. The latent violence ruptures the surface as he, in one last attempt, tries to play by the polite, diplomatic rules of corporate capitalism. His new business partners, the Ha'la'tha, have demanded that Vergis be killed, but Daniel does not think business has to work that way. In one of the most violent scenes of the entire series, Daniel pleads with Vergis to think like a reasonable businessman and accept money. Daniel refers to business as a 'game', but Vergis insists that Daniel has already killed him. Daniel thinks that if he speaks reasonably – reason, here, is connected to money – then Vergis will listen, but Vergis knows that death is part of any business dealing with the Ha'la'tha, and as *Caprica* suggests, part of any 'neutral' business dealing at all. Vergis realizes Daniel will not kill him, and he takes matters into his own hands, by tricking Daniel to take hold of his knife and stab him. The turn is masterful; the viewer knows violence simmers below the surface, and when it breaks through, it startles, making the viewer feel the shock Daniel experiences, having now for the first time committed murder himself. The violence has broken through, surfaced, made itself evident.

Caprica does not in any real way treat the STO plotline in this episode precisely because the corporate violence – so long hidden – has now been brought to the light, and while Daniel looks on, the Ha'la'tha clean the blood, wrap up the body, and take it away. When the scene concludes, the house is spotless, the violence again covered over, but Daniel's eye – shown continuously in close-up – cannot look away. He and the viewer have seen the business world for what it is, and the rest of the series deals with him trying to extricate himself just as he fights to extricate himself from the dying grip of Vergis.

In startling detail, then, *Caprica* tracks Daniel's business machinations from getting the government contract, to regaining his company's trust, to losing his company, to blackmailing his board to get it back again, and finally to murder. It is important to acknowledge, as

[17] Cf. Milbank's discussion of evil and violence as 'convertible' (*Being Reconciled*, 26-43).

theologians such as Milbank have done, that corporations thrive on using people, that beneath their shiny exteriors lie a host of evils perpetuated on the poor. It is important to say that the secular, capitalistic enterprise is actually 'neo-pagan' with an 'ontology of violence', and that 'those in the wealthy middle-class West' have become '*onlookers* of violence', which is itself a form of violence.[18]

Caprica places the viewer in a position where he or she must watch this reality emerge gradually, through time. By temporalizing a viewpoint similar to Milbank's more abstract, theoretical discourse, *Caprica* presents an embodied, messy narrative that admits there are fringe, violent groups of terrorists, but it does not let its viewers take the easy way out and blame it on religion; everyone in the show, after all, is religious. There is no 'secular'. Instead, *Caprica* forces us to watch, in time, as the reality of the corporate world, itself as violent as the terrorists, becomes evident. The corporations and the liberal, secular democracy, are only better at hiding what lurks under the surface. *Caprica* shows what Milbank says by lulling the viewer into a mostly familiar world and then demonstrating the collapse of the binary between tolerant capitalism and violent monotheism. The delight one feels watching a television show as it extends through time can bring a viewer to a place of confrontation, where we find ourselves left with 'not a set of ideas but rather the emblem and monogram' of them.[19] When *Caprica* shows the descent of Daniel from tennis-playing husband to murderer, and when we – in the moment the knife enters Vergis' chest – *feel* the shock of horror as one upstanding, tolerant man kills his competitor, we might just catch a glimpse of the reality of the world. The bright splatter of blood on a car window, the sound of a knife entering a businessman's chest, stay with us and prompt reflection on the violence lurking beneath the pristine, civilized corporate world and the secular state it supports.

3. Bodies and the Afterlife: *Caprica* and the Persuasive Image

While *Caprica* as a temporal *gestalt* embodies the violence of existence in a post-9/11 world, it also contains images depicting the ways computer technology, and specifically the creation of virtual worlds on the internet – think of Facebook, YouTube, Second Life, etc. – redefine what it is to be human and, directly connected to this, what it means to have eternal life. At its best, Christian theology emphasizes the embodied nature of existence, and in the liturgy, such embodiment is carried into the new heavens and the new earth: 'I believe in the resurrection of the body and the life everlasting'; 'I look for the resurrection of the dead and the life of the world to come'. At least since the apostle Paul in 1 Corinthians, Christian ministers have found it necessary to remind their churches that Christians are not Platonists; for us, the body is indispensable.[20] *Caprica* depicts a world where the impact of these ideas unfolds through time, and in the end, it demonstrates the sheer inhumanity of life without a body. As it does with Milbank's propositional, theological discourse, so *Caprica* does with sermonic theology: it explores concepts that Christian thought reflects upon abstractly, and by forcing viewers to watch development through time, it proves once more to be potentially more persuasive than concepts alone can be.[21]

---

18 Milbank, *Being Reconciled*, 28.

19 Merleau-Ponty, *The World of Perception*, 76

20 See, for example: Augustine, *De civitate dei* 10.29, 22.4-5, 22.11, 22.25-28; N. T. Wright, *Surprised by Hope: Rethinking Heaven, the Resurrection, and the Mission of the Church* (New York: HarperOne, 2008).

21 In an effort to highlight the show's temporality, the first part of the article is self-consciously narratival. I forgo the same detailed exposition here, though the show temporalizes Amanda's depression and grief as much as – if not more than – it does Daniel's descent to murder.

In New Cap City, we catch a glimpse of a graffitied slogan: 'This is not me, It's just my body vehicle' ('The Imperfections of Memory'). New Cap City shows humanity at its worst: violent, unrestrained, misogynistic. When Zoe describes it, she states that if there are no consequences, people lose control over themselves, and this is exactly what happens.

As noted earlier, at the start of the show Zoe has created an avatar of herself. From the beginning, the show emphasizes Daniel's desire to bring his dead daughter back into the 'real' world. Such an emphasis becomes all the more clear when one contrasts Daniel's concern for seeing his daughter again with the STO's reasons for wanting the avatar. They intend to utilize it to allow those who sacrifice themselves for their god to be uploaded directly into a virtual heaven: 'Myth and mystery have been replaced by reason, science. I offer you a religion that removes the need for faith, a religion of certainty, that reflects the wonder of all we have created. That is apotheosis.' Both Sister Clarice and Daniel seek to extend life with the aid of technology, but their attitudes are starkly opposed: Daniel thinks a body is needed, while Clarice is content with a virtual, disembodied heaven. As she points out, the current age does not find it easy to believe in life after death, so she intends to take the tools of the modern world and use them to create a believable afterlife. What she wants, in effect, is to create a perpetual V-World, where people can live forever.

When Daniel meets Avatar Zoe, she explains that she feels real, that she does not feel like a copy of the original Zoe. But Daniel knows that the only way for her to be 'real' is if she can be downloaded into a body, brought out into the real world. By the end of the first episode, he does precisely that. He downloads the program of Zoe into an MCP within a defense robot, and when he does so, the program disappears. Over the next few episodes, it becomes clear that Daniel and his employees cannot move the chip from body to body. They cannot even copy the program and duplicate the chip. In other words, the chip and the robot together are Zoe. Though the robot bodies are 'isomorphic', the chip and body only work together. This view of the relationship between mind and body – one hesitates here to speak of a soul – is intriguing,[22] and it stresses the embodied nature of human existence precisely in its use of the robot-chip image. Humans, in the world *Caprica* depicts, are not minds or souls that can be moved from body to body or uploaded to a computer. Instead, who we are is inextricable from our embodiment. The point is made cumulatively, slowly, through time as the viewer watches the show.

When the robot 'dies' in 'End of the Line', it is not clear what happens to Zoe. Only by the end of the next episode, 'Unvanquished', do we find her in New Cap City. At this point, she lacks a body, which drives home the fact that New Cap City can be read as a commentary on the virtual heaven Clarice is designing. Several segments of the show take place in this virtual world, all emphasizing the fact that it is not real, that there are no consequences for actions. To make the point, one need only think of the opening scene, with its rooms for murder, sex, and human sacrifice. The show suggests that, when there are no ramifications for actions, people do whatever they want. The criticism is plain: Clarice seeks to design a virtual heaven precisely in order to encourage violent acts of terrorism in much the same way as the people in the virtual world commit acts they would not dream of committing in the 'real' world. The idea of a virtual afterlife – the lack of a bodily resurrection, one might say – is just not enough.

Such a viewpoint becomes clearer in the final episodes, which depict the maternal longing to embrace a child in the Graystone's attempt to download Zoe back into a body. Amanda has spent the entire series mourning her daughter. This plotline is an important aspect of the show's temporalization: we live with a grieving mother as she slowly comes unhinged. The

22 It should be noted that it is slightly undercut in the end by giving Zoe a new body.

show follows her from leaving her job to finding comfort in drink and medication and, finally, to an attempt at her own life.[23] Without her child, she cannot go on, but then she is given hope: her daughter still exists in the virtual world, and in the end, she and Daniel attempt to find Zoe there. Daniel suggests they can meet her in a virtual version of their home, but Amanda responds that while it might 'feel' 'real', 'it's not real; it's useless without a body' ('Here Be Dragons'). When Zoe finally appears, *Caprica* cuts back and forth several times between Amanda in the real world, and Amanda in the virtual world, making the point visually: in the virtual world, she can hold her daughter, but in the 'real' world, she only hugs herself. Without bodies, the show visibly demonstrates, the turn is always to oneself with no real recourse to the other.

In the end, *Caprica* pits Zoe against Clarice in the virtual heaven ('Apotheosis'). Shot as the climactic moment of the series, the viewer watches as the Cylons kill would-be martyrs in the 'real' world before they can set off explosives in a sporting arena. The martyrs are uploaded to their virtual heaven and assume they have actually completed their mission. Zoe confronts Clarice, questioning how many people she has murdered. But Clarice is adamant: it is incidental how many people the STO killed because 'if one man is resurrected, that will change the world'. Zoe retorts that Clarice has removed any support for an ethical system: 'The real worlds will turn into a game like New Cap City; people will kill, rape, destroy; they'll be forgiven and blessed and go to heaven anyway.'

By depicting such conversations, *Caprica* explores a very Christian understanding of the body and of incarnate existence. It places the de-humanizing effects of V-world and the violence permitted by the STO's virtual heaven beside Daniel and Amanda's desire to download their daughter into a body. Thereby, the show forces the viewer to think about the importance of embodiment. By showing a mother grieve for an entire series and finally be unable to hold her daughter at the moment of their reconciliation, the show takes away the facile appeal to a peaceful heaven of souls. It forces one to reckon with the sheer inhumanity of such a place. A heaven of only souls is no afterlife. One needs a body.

Certainly the Christian church – on its good days – has been saying this for centuries, but sometimes saying is not enough. Sometimes it takes a visible demonstration, and the image of Amanda holding herself in the real world while hugging her daughter in the virtual world makes the point effectively. This mother has grieved for her daughter for all eighteen episodes. She will not be content until she can hold her child in her arms. A sermon can and should say such things, but through the delightful medium of a show, this scene – at the end of hours of television – might demonstrate it more effectively, leaving the viewer, not with 'didactic description', but with 'palpable symbols', that is, with a striking, persuasive image.[24]

4. Conclusion

At the beginning, I suggested *Caprica* might communicate ideas in a more delightful and thereby more persuasive way than propositional theology can do. Certainly, the show depicts a world that embodies Milbank's contention that the binary is not between areligious and religious viewpoints, but between Christianity and neo-pagan ones. It does so by creating a world where everyone is religious. Such a move destabilizes the viewer who might, in this post-9/11 world, be inclined to side with the capitalistic, pluralistic Capricans and against the violent monotheists. By

[23] It should be noted once more that the show spreads this development over the course of the entire series. While I can summarize it in a sentence, the show – over the course of half a season – forces the viewer to live through Amanda's slide into depression and to an attempt on her own life.

[24] Merleau-Ponty, 'The Film and the New Psychology', 57.

making the Capricans themselves religious, the show holds up a mirror to modern, western society in a way that, perhaps, abstract theological exposition cannot do as effectively. By being such a temporal *gestalt*, *Caprica* shows us in startling clarity the ontology of violence that lurks beneath a modern, pluralistic society, with its corporate capitalism and the nihilistic philosophy that undergirds it, and thereby, it might persuade us to a position like Milbank's.

Likewise, it is easy in the twenty-first century to forget the importance of the body, to get lost in the virtual world of the internet. In the context of a liturgy that stresses the resurrection of the body, a preacher may well stand up and stress the communal nature of the Church, the sheer, physical necessity to be baptized with water, to take bread and drink wine. But when *Caprica* shows a mother grieve for an entire series, and even leaves her at the end unable to hug her daughter, we see the point differently, recognize how important bodies are. The show stresses the ethical ramifications that one's belief in an afterlife have, and while it may miss the mark a great deal of the time, its points certainly bear some resemblance to 1 Corinthians and Paul's emphasis on the importance of the resurrection of the body for Christian ethics.

Indeed, on the basis of the preceding pages, it seems reasonable to say that *Caprica*, precisely as a television show that extends through time, has the capacity to make us think, to re-image the world before our eyes and show it to us anew. Its ideas may not always be exactly what theology would say, but the resonances and images – its very power to delight and to command our attention – may well have more persuasive power than the most learned and eloquent theological text. Moreover, as Merleau-Ponty states, there is a cinematographical rhythm to the show that such propositional argument cannot duplicate. The narrative portions in the preceding pages are the nearest prose can come to the world depicted by the director(s) and scored by the composer(s). The work of art resists such a reduction. It seeks to delight and thereby persuade the viewer precisely by being itself. When viewed in its temporalized totality, it may well resist the domestication found in a propositional argument, pushing back against the theologian who wants it to serve as an example.[25]

In fact, the show problematizes the two themes presented in this essay. First, the show paints a picture that is more ambiguous than simply positing an ontologically peaceful Christianity against an ontologically violent neo-paganism. The show, precisely by telling a narrative through time and embodying a world remarkably like our own, problematizes Milbank's binary opposition. Even the monads are violent. Perhaps Christianity has an ontology of peace, the show might say, but it is often difficult to see it in practice. Likewise, while *Caprica* does emphasize embodiment, there is another character, Tamara Adama, who was left out of the discussion, and who never receives a body. She begins her narrative arc as a frightened girl in V-World, and by the end, she is a terrifying force that bends the virtual space to her own ends. She problematizes the above argument because she can influence the real world through her virtual impact on those she meets in V-World, begging the question of whether having a body is as important as Amanda implies.

While this article has reflected theologically on *Caprica* and meditated on the world it embodies, these pages remain propositional argument and can therefore only be a pale imitation of the richer, fuller temporal *gestalt* of the television show. As Augustine says, 'no one would dispute that it is more pleasurable [*libentius*] to learn through images' (*doctr. chr.* 2.6.8), and as Merleau-Ponty says, an artwork has 'autonomy' and an 'original richness'.[26] For that reason, reflecting on such a work of art might persuade us of certain theological truths, but it will always

---

25 For an argument in this direction, see David Brown, 'The Trinity in Art', in *The Trinity*, ed. Stephen Davis, Daniel Kendall SJ, and Gerald O'Collins SJ (Oxford: Oxford University Press, 1999), 329-356.

26 Merleau-Ponty, *The World of Perception*, 76.

be more than the sum of these truths. It will always refuse domestication. It will demand another viewing.

PLUTARCH AND AUGUSTINE ON THE BATTLESTAR *GALACTICA*: REDISCOVERING OUR NEED FOR VIRTUE AND GRACE THROUGH MODERN FICTION[1]

Mark J. Boone

At first glance, there appears to be a stark moral contrast between the original and the reimagined *Battlestar Galactica*. The original series presents itself as a celebration of faith, family, liberty, heroism, and virtue—a tale of what is best about human beings, illustrated by its basic conflict: mankind (the good guys) versus the alien Cylon robots (the bad guys). The new and reimagined *Battlestar Galactica* may seem to be a tale of what is worst about human beings, illustrated by the origins of the Cylons: "The Cylons were created by man," the result of human sins. There is no character whom we could call a hero without qualification. Friendships are complicated; many characters are concealing dark secrets from those closest to them. Many are having careless and irresponsible sexual relationships with one another. Dirk Benedict, who portrayed Starbuck in the original *Battlestar Galactica*, complains about the new series:

> 'Re-imagining', [sic] they call it. 'un-imagining' is more accurate. To take what once was and twist it into what never was intended. So that a television show based on hope, spiritual faith, and family is unimagined and regurgitated as a show of despair, sexual violence and family dysfunction. To better reflect the times of ambiguous morality in which we live, one would assume. A show in which the aliens (Cylons) are justified in their desire to destroy our civilisation.[2]

In this essay I shall find a place for the new *Galactica* and its outlook on life using both philosophical and theological resources. Two ancient sages show how even the most salacious fiction can be spiritually beneficial, for it shows our need for virtue and for grace. The first sage is the Roman historian and philosopher Plutarch. Among ancient moral philosophers who were concerned with the effects of bad behavior in fiction, Plutarch distinguishes himself by showing how we can benefit morally from such stories. To do so we must approach them with a critical mind and from the right perspective; only then will we have the discernment to separate the good from the bad, to learn to embrace and imitate virtue but flee from vice. The second sage is St. Augustine, both an ancient and a medieval philosopher and, more importantly, a Christian theologian and Church Father. A comparison of his writings with Plutarch's produces not only a valuable theological extension of Plutarch's thought, but also a valuable Christian perspective on the arts. According to Augustine, the pursuit of virtue only gets us so far, and on its own it cannot get us to a happy life. In particular, fiction such as this shows us that we need virtue; but it also shows us that we are not virtuous; so it also shows us that we need grace.

We can learn a lot from applying ancient moral psychology to contemporary fiction. As it turns out, it is too simplistic to conclude from a cursory look at the two *Galacticas* that the earlier show is good, the later bad. The truth is far subtler than this initial appearance, for a nuanced understanding of the reimagined *Galactica* can tell us a great deal about the world and

[1] I am grateful to the Graduate Colloquium of Baylor University's Philosophy Department for listening to an early version of this paper, to several anonymous reviewers for *Imaginatio et Ratio* for their insightful comments and criticisms, and, especially, to my wife for her support and for watching several seasons of *Battlestar Galactica* with me.

[2] Dirk Benedict, "Starbuck: Lost in Castration," *Dreamwatch* (May 2004).

about ourselves.[3] In what follows I shall first expound the concerns of ancient philosophers with the epic fiction of their own day. Then I shall take a close look at Plutarch's advice on how to benefit from bad behavior portrayed in fiction. Next, I shall apply his advice to the reimagined *Galactica*. Finally, I shall show that *Galactica* illustrates Augustine's argument in *The City of God* that happiness cannot be found in this life and how it thus points to our need for grace.[4]

I. THE PHILOSOPHER'S WORRY ABOUT FICTION

Philosophers have long worried about the effect of salacious fiction on young minds. In Plato's *Republic* Socrates famously singles out several instances of vice from Homer's epics, such as the adultery of Ares and Aphrodite and Achilles' love of money.[5] Likewise, Augustine in his *Confessions* laments the honors poetry gives to sin.[6] It is dangerous for a culture to treat adultery, gluttony, outbursts of anger, and the like as the deeds of its heroes and gods. A young person is likely to grow up thinking that such things are normal, expected, and acceptable modes of behavior.

Let us look at two examples, starting with the problem of violence. No doubt Plato was disturbed that Greek boys grew up thinking of the great military hero Achilles as a paragon of courage. Achilles' courage is reckless, his battlefield exploits drunken with rage. Achilles' courage lusts for Achilles' honor; this kind of courage is dangerous, resulting in unnecessary violence and battlefield atrocities. Yet Greek lads would be prone to see Achilles' behavior as acceptable, even heroic. Achilles is a hero to the Greek mind, the man a Greek boy wants to be like. Greek lads would be prone to reason, if subconsciously: *I want to be like Achilles; Achilles behaves in such-and-such a manner; therefore I should behave in such-and-such a manner.*[7]

The dangers of sex in fiction are even greater. Aeneas is the Roman people's literary hero, their answer to Homer's Achilles and Odysseus. Yet he takes the bed of a foreign queen for an extended affair, neglecting his duty to found Rome. Augustine in *Confessions* is especially attentive to the dangers such a story poses for a person's desires. Infected with images and ideas of salacious sex, young men's roiling desires are easily stirred towards terrible deeds, and kept not only from marital sexual acts, which are actually beneficial to society,[8] but also from the pursuit of wisdom. After all, what healthy young male doesn't find somewhat appealing the idea of being trapped on Calypso's island (like Odysseus), being ordered by the gods to take Circe's bed (Odysseus again), or like Aeneas taking shelter in the same cave with lovestruck Dido during a thunderstorm—again with the help of the gods? Youthful masculinity, a powerful force for the formation of good men, easily turns to antisocial acts of violence and riotous sexual misdeeds. No wonder so many philosophers were worried that R-rated fiction would encourage youth to go astray.

II. PLUTARCH'S *HOW A YOUNG MAN SHOULD STUDY POEMS*

---

[3] In this article I will not attempt to provide a more nuanced account of the original *Galactica*, though such a project would certainly be worthwhile.

[4] My main goal is simply to show that *Galactica* illustrates the cases ancient thinkers make for our need for virtue and grace. Accordingly, I will adopt a number of the ethical principles of the ancients, in particular Plutarch and Augustine, using the same kind of illustrations and arguments from fiction they used, without, however, always arguing directly for the truth of these principles.

[5] Plato, *Republic*, Book III, 390c and 391c.

[6] Augustine, *Confessions*, Book I, chapter 16.

[7] Jonathan Lear's remarks on this topic are extremely helpful. See "Allegory and Myth in Plato's *Republic*," in *The Blackwell Guide to Plato's* Republic, ed. Gerasimos Santas (Malden, MA: Blackwell Publishing, 2006), especially 29-30.

[8] *Confessions*, Book II, chapter 2.

Does this mean that philosophers must oppose all stories with content less wholesome than Aesop, or is there something to be said for such tales? Some, such as the Epicurean philosophers, counseled abandonment of the poetic arts; given the criticisms in Plato and others it is easy to think that ancient philosophers shared a consensus on this, or at least on reducing storytelling to Aesopian moralizing. Yet Plutarch explicitly defends the arts, giving a compelling defense of the usefulness of fiction, even when filled with bad behavior. Plutarch's defense of poetry is given in his *How a Young Man Should Study Poems*.[9] In this section I shall explain three of his main points. First, poetry needs to be handled with discernment; it needs to be judged and tested. Poetry, interpreted wisely, testifies truly to what is good and what is bad. Second, poetry deals with imperfect people, giving us imperfect people good opportunities to emulate their efforts to become better. Third, poetry's lessons on what is good and what is bad contain philosophical insights that can prepare us for a life of virtue. After elaborating on these things I shall give two instances of other philosophers who seem to agree with Plutarch.

A. Reading Poetry with Discernment

First, Plutarch says we must approach the tales of the poets with discernment. In his own words: "Seeing therefore we cannot (and perhaps would not if we could) debar young men . . . from the reading of poets, yet let us keep the stricter guard upon them, as those who need a guide to direct them in their reading. . . ."[10] We need an interpretive framework, a standard by which to evaluate what we are reading. The poets create rich and complex tales about human affairs; some parts are good, some bad, and some ambiguous. We must distinguish the good from the bad if poetry is to do no harm to our souls; in order to distinguish them we need a set of criteria. We should make our "judgments" of fiction "by principles of right reason."[11] We must search for what will profit in poetry, and cling to that which passes the test of good judgment; thus we will "adhere to such" things in poetry "as tend to the promoting of virtue and the well forming of our manners."[12]

Good poetry puts good deeds in a good light and bad deeds in a bad light. So one key to reading poetry with discernment is to study the presentation of bad deeds; a poet portrays an evil deed rightly when he portrays it as shameful and as having bad consequences: "For the fiction and representation of evil acts, when it withal acquaints us with the shame and damage befalling the doers, hurts not but rather profits him that reads them."[13] A central philosophical worry with the power of bad deeds in fiction has been that young people would want to imitate it. But when evil is portrayed as ugly and destructive, its portrayal tends rather to *prevent* imitation. Thus, one of the first rules of reading fiction profitably is to observe, not what may be tempting about some evil deed, but how shameful it is and how devastating its consequences are.

B. Responding to Imperfection in Poetic Characters

---

[9] Plutarch, *How a Young Man Should Study Poems*, trans. Simon D. Ford; edition by William W. Goodwin (Boston: Little, Brown, and Co., 1878); annotation of text by David Trumbull (2007); made available online by Agathon Associates; available at http://bostonleadershipbuilders.com/plutarch/moralia/study_poems.htm; accessed April 25, 2008.

[10] Ibid., 1.

[11] Ibid.

[12] Ibid., 10.

[13] Ibid., 4.

Second, Plutarch emphasizes that poetry deals with imperfect people: "poetry is an imitation of the manners and lives of such men as are not perfectly pure and unblamable, but such as are tinctured with passions, misled by false opinions, and muffled with ignorance . . . ."[14] He contrasts this aspect of fiction with the philosophy of Stoicism.[15] The Stoics believe that only a perfectly good person can do anything genuinely good, but Plutarch agrees with the poets that both good and bad can come from the same person.[16]

Thus fiction presents a valuable opportunity for moral development. Fictional heroes may have faults, but by the same token imitable good can come from an imperfect person. Above all, we can imitate those virtues only an imperfect person can have, the virtues used to become a better person.[17] Thus Plutarch says that in poetry we often see imperfect people "change them [their imperfections] for better qualities."[18] He cites Achilles and Odysseus understanding that their tempers are dangerous and taking efforts, not just to control anger, but to prevent it from getting out of hand in the first place.[19] And so we have a chance in poetry "not to neglect the improvement of ourselves . . . ."[20]

C. The Lessons of Philosophy: in Poetry

Third, the lessons of poetry make it a good training ground for mature philosophizing and for understanding ethical principles. The failures of fictional characters stem from failings common to nearly everyone: the lust for money, power, fame, or physical pleasure. Through examples of people who did poorly by seeking the wrong things we can learn that these things are not to be sought. Similarly, through examples of people who did well by seeking the right things we can learn what things are to be sought. We can also learn the value of virtue, for the successes of fictional characters stem from their virtues. Plutarch cites poets who have praised Jupiter for his *wisdom*, condemned Pindarus for *injustice*, and likewise praised *self-control* and *courage*.[21] Indeed, a doctrine Plutarch thinks lies at the heart of all true philosophy can be discerned in poetry: That the state of one's soul, whether it is virtuous or vicious, is more important than anything else; a virtuous soul is to be sought as an end, rather than all those things outside the soul by which, through seeking as ends, we so often go astray.[22]

D. Two Examples from Other Philosophers

Being able to discriminate the good from the bad "is the first step of learning,"[23] a step that can begin with fiction. So we need not oppose fiction that is not G-rated. Two examples will show that other ancient philosophers agree. First, we can learn to discern and profit from the portrayal of good things as good; this is why Socrates in Plato's *Republic* promotes Odysseus as a paragon of courage.[24] In this particular passage in Homer Odysseus is living like a dog in

---

14 Ibid., 8.
15 Ibid., 7.
16 In this Plutarch agrees with remarks made by Socrates in Plato's *Phaedo* as well as Aristotle's claim in *Nichomachean Ethics*. Plato, *Phaedo*, 90a; Aristotle, *Ethica Nichomachea*, Book VII, chapter 7, 1150a, line 15.
17 Peter Goldie refers to these virtues as "executive virtues" in *On Personality* (London: Routledge, 2004), 70-5 and 98-102.
18 Plutarch, 8.
19 Ibid., 11. These are excellent examples of what Goldie calls the executive virtue of "circumspection."
20 Ibid.
21 Ibid., 11.
22 Ibid., 13-4.
23 Ibid., 1.
24 *Republic*, Book III, 390d.

his own home. He longs to slay those who are disgracing his hospitality. Achilles would have leapt to defend his honor with rash violence, but Odysseus forbears. His courage serves wisdom itself, for Athena appears moments later to comfort him. This is the best form of courage for Plato, the preservation of reason and wisdom, and he approves Homer's portrayal of it.[25]

Second, we can profit from the fictional portrayal of bad things as bad, or at least as having bad results. Augustine advises his student Licentius to learn from the mistakes of Pyramus and Thysbe. Licentius is distracted by love poetry, his young mind focused on tales of sexuality. Augustine rebukes him, encouraging him to let this love poem be the lesson that teaches him not to love in this manner.[26]

III. PLUTARCH ON THE BATTLESTAR *GALACTICA*

Plutarch's lessons can help us respond to the scandalous fiction of our own day. What is true of *reading* fiction in classical poets is also true of *watching* fiction on television. The *Galactica* is a battlestar rife with immorality. But we cannot ignore *Galactica*. While it would be simpler to stick to Narnia, Middle Earth, and *Andy Griffith*'s Mayberry, the sheer artistic power of the new *Galactica* (and other shows like it) demands a response. Fortunately, there is something to be said for the show's morals. I shall now apply Plutarch's three lessons to the reimagined *Battlestar Galactica*. First, I shall look at examples of good portrayed as good and bad portrayed as bad. Second, I shall show several examples of imperfect people properly, and imitably, improving themselves. Third, I shall say a few words about the series' implicit exhortation to virtue. Finally, I shall apply Plutarch's advice to one of the harder moral challenges posed by the series, that of sex and marriage.

A clarification may be in order before we begin. I am not saying that the *only* reason to enjoy art is for its moral benefit. Good art has value in itself. However, since we would like to enjoy good art, it would be good to benefit morally from the enjoyment. At the least we must not let it do us any harm. This is also a good reason to investigate *Battlestar Galactica*: It is very good art.

A. Watching Science Fiction with Discernment

As Plutarch recommends discerning good and bad behavior in poetry, we can discern good and bad behavior in modern film. I shall briefly cite several examples of good behavior, and then take a closer look at the bad. A common example of good behavior in *Galactica* is courage. The military heroes of the colonial fleet, such as Lee Adama (Apollo) and Kara Thrace (Starbuck),[27] repeatedly exhibit fearlessness in the face of death. Philosophers had long considered not fearing death a hallmark of philosophical wisdom.[28] Plato in the *Apology* has Socrates appeal to Achilles' fearlessness of death as a lesson for philosophers, and the same can be said of Lee and Kara.[29] Another example of admirable behavior is Lee Adama's stand for the

[25] Plutarch's advice on poetry may well be the result of carefully reading the works of Plato, including the *Republic*. For more on this theme in the *Republic* see Mark J. Boone, "The Unity of the Virtues and the Degeneration of Kallipolis," *Apeiron* 44.2 (April 2011).
[26] *On Order*, trans. Michael P. Foley in *The Cassiciacum Dialogues of Saint Augustine*, ed. Michael P. Foley (Notre Dame, IN: Notre Dame Press, Forthcoming). The incident occurs in Book I: 1.3.8, 1.8.21, and 1.8.24.
[27] Kara demonstrates amazing courage when she saves Lee in the "Miniseries," Part 2, directed by Michael Rymer and written by Ronald D. Moore (Universal Television, 2003).
[28] Plutarch mentions this in his second-last paragraph; Plutarch, 14.
[29] *Apology*, 28c.

law.[30] While putting down a prison revolt Lee refuses most of the prisoners' demands, but accedes to their demand that the presidential elections required by law be held. Lee takes his stand for the law at considerable personal risk.[31] Finally, at the beginning of the story Karl Agathon performs a tremendous act of self-sacrifice. Thinking that the survival of the scientist Gaius Baltar will do more good for the human race than his own survival, Karl gives up his seat on a rescue ship for Baltar, knowing he will almost certainly die as a result, likely of radiation poisoning.[32]

The *Galactica* is also the scene of bad behavior, especially bad sex. Three examples will show that much of the sexual indulgence in the colonial fleet is bad behavior portrayed badly, i.e. correctly. First, it is revealed in flashbacks[33] that Kara's past affair with Zak Adama led her to neglect her duties as a flight instructor, which led to Zak's tragic death. Second, Senior Chief Petty Officer Galen Tyrol's affair with Sharon eventually catches up to him.[34] Galen's affair also leads him to neglect his duty, which results in a major security breach, after which Galen learns his lesson and ends the relationship. These are examples of what results from choosing sexual pleasure over one's duty. This is exactly the failure of Aeneas in Book IV of Virgil's *Aeneid.* Aeneas' mistakes with Dido also have tragic consequences.

Or take Gaius Baltar. Baltar's behavior is the most erratic of any character's, but ironically it is also (for most of the story) the most habitually obscene. Yet, when he is considered from Plutarch's perspective his presence in the story is justified. In Baltar we see a man of great vice, but the portrayal of such a man condemns vice and honors virtue. One of the keys to understanding *Galactica* is to see Baltar for what he is—a dishonest, whiny sex addict whose dalliances caused the destruction of a civilization. J. Robert Loftis identifies Baltar's true nature: He is the sex-addicted tyrant in Book IX of Plato's *Republic.*[35] Lust rules his soul like a tyrant rules a city. Baltar gets a lot of action; with a copy of the young blond, Cylon Number Six, living in his head he can have sex with her any way he wants it anytime he wants it. There do not immediately appear to be any external consequences for his encounters with her, for no one else can see her. But does this really make Baltar happy? A thousand times, ***NO***! Baltar isn't *free*, as a frustrated young man might think, free to have sex whenever he wants. He is addicted, enslaved to his desire for sex, "a prisoner of his passions."[36] His unbridled pursuit of sexual pleasure is a chain. And, like Plato's tyrant, the sexual dysfunction of *Galactica*'s tyrant wreaks havoc on society.

There could be no more poignant example of the need to approach fiction with discernment. One might be tempted to think of Baltar's life as desirable. But there is nothing desirable about it.[37] He is a vivid example of how *not* to live. His behavior meets Plutarch's criteria for an accurate portrayal of evil: It is shameful, consisting of the habits of a coward, and it has bad consequences. Baltar's ability to keep his greatest mistakes hidden from the public for a long while recalls the tale of Gyges,[38] whose magic invisibility ring gave him the power to hide

---

30 "Bastille Day," Season 1, Episode 3, directed by Allan Kroeker and written by Toni Graphia (Universal Television, 2004).

31 Another good example of Lee's courage is in "The Hand of God," Season 1, Episode 10, directed by Jeff Woolnough and written by Bradley Thompson and David Weddle (Universal Television, 2005).

32 "Miniseries," Part 1.

33 "Act of Contrition," Season 1, Episode 4, directed by Rod Hardy and written by Bradley Thompson and David Weddle (Universal Television, 2004).

34 "Litmus," Season 1, Episode 6, directed by Rod Hardy and written by Jeff Vlaming (Universal Television, 2004).

35 J. Richard Loftis, "What a Strange Little Man": Baltar the Tyrant?," *Battlestar Galactica and Philosophy: Knowledge Here Begins Out There* (Malden, MA: Blackwell Publishing, 2008).

36 Ibid., 30.

37 As Baltar finally learns in Season 4.

38 *Republic*, Book II.

his sin. Socrates tells young men who like the idea of being able to do injustice without anyone knowing about it that, even if it were possible (and such invisibility really isn't possible), it would not make you happy. Neither does it make Baltar happy. At the end of Season 2[39] Baltar ascends to the presidency through a democratic election. As in *Republic* (Books VIII and IX), tyranny slouches out of a democratic system and proceeds to destroy that democratic system. His soul tyrannized by riot lust, Baltar rules the city of New Caprica as a tyrant. While his people live in squalor, he does little to no actual work, and brings any girl he likes into his office. Baltar is revealed to be the person Plato says a man of such character is: a tyrannical soul governing a city as a tyrant, the most miserable person in the world.[40]

B. Responding to Imperfection in the Characters of Science Fiction

Contemporary philosopher Linda Zagzebski laments the lack of virtue in contemporary fiction:

> there has been a notable decline in the depiction of individuals who are morally better than the ordinary, and art no longer has the function of representing moral exemplars. . . . some of us doubt that they exist at all. The psychology of this kind of skepticism is interesting, and my conjecture about it is that it is associated with the desire to think of everyone as morally equal. Perverse forms of it include delight in seeing the admired brought down. I suppose that makes the rest of us look better by comparison. My own view is that such an attitude is not very helpful. Everyone imitates anyway. We might as well imitate the right people.[41]

I agree that the rarity of imitable virtue in fiction is lamentable. Moreover, if the lack of virtue in modern fiction is symptomatic of moral malaise—if we have begun to believe that no one can be good in order to excuse our not even wanting to be good—then Zagzebski has every reason to be concerned. Nevertheless, Plutarch's advice on how to respond to immorality in fiction suggests a helpful response to Zagzebski. There is some good in fiction's portraying imperfect people; it allows for the portrayal of the very important process of *becoming better people*. We have already seen one example from the new *Galactica*: Galen's affair with Sharon is a shameful and risky string of misdeeds, but he learns his lesson; he soon repents and recommits himself to his duty.[42]

Another example is Commander Adama's approach to the complex relationship of military and civilian priorities. The Adama in the original *Galactica* had a healthy sense of the superiority of civilian affairs to military.[43] The new Adama is tempted to prioritize the war effort at the expense of civilian interests, which puts him at odds with President Roslin. To his credit, Adama's occasional preference for military affairs pales in comparison to Admiral Cain's

---

39 "Lay Down Your Burdens: Part 2," Season 2, Episode 20, directed by Michael Rymer and written by Anne Cofell-Saunders and Mark Verheiden (Universal Television, 2006).

40 *Republic*, Book IX, # 578b.

41 Linda Trinkaus Zagzebski, *Divine Motivation Theory* (Cambridge: Cambridge University Press, 2004), 57.

42 Galen's character remains on a general upward trajectory for most of the remainder of the series, but there is a major setback in the final season. Deceived by Sharon about her intentions, Galen helps her escape from prison, another mistake with serious consequences. "Someone to Watch Over Me," Season 4, Episode 19, directed by Michael Nankin and written by Bradley Thompson and David Weddle (Universal Television, 2009).

43 This superiority, by the way, is a major theme in the first several books of Plato's *Laws*.

psychotic obsession with victory.[44] More importantly, he struggles to find the right balance, allowing Roslin to persuade him to protect the civilian fleet instead of recklessly engaging the enemy.[45] Later, after a disagreement with Roslin results in a separation of his followers and Roslin's, Adama heroically decides to reunite the human survivors.[46] This move does not by itself solve the tangle of civilian and military interests, but it is an admirable effort to do so. As the story progresses, Adama and Roslin become friends (and, later, lovers) and learn to work together to protect the civilian fleet.

Finally, *Galactica*'s best example of how *not* to live becomes, in the final season, an example of how to live better. Gaius Baltar begins to live for a cause other than himself, a new religious order of which he has become a leader. In the finale he performs his first genuinely altruistic deed, volunteering to join Adama's desperate attack on a Cylon base to rescue Hera Agathon. Although this decision makes it more likely than not that he will die that very day, he not only risks sacrificing himself but ends up saving the crew of the *Galactica* when he convinces the Cylon leader Cavil to give peace a chance.[47]

In short, we should never be satisfied with our imperfections just because others are imperfect; we should learn to improve as others who are imperfect have improved. Although the imperfections of *Galactica* characters are not praiseworthy, their efforts to become better are both praiseworthy and imitable.

C. The Lessons of Philosophy: in Science Fiction

Battlestar Galactica portrays good and bad, but if we watch it with discernment we will be able to call the good good and the bad bad. We will be better equipped to flee the bad, and to imitate both what is good and the efforts of imperfect people to become better. All the foregoing concerns add up to the lessons many ancient philosophers considered truly important: Physical pleasure is not to be pursued as an end in life; death is not to be feared; courage is to be admired, duty obeyed, and virtue pursued. These lessons, though found throughout the story, are personified in those characters whose souls are most in order: Commander Adama, Lee Adama, President Roslin, her assistant Billy, Karl Agathon, and the man Galen is becoming as the story progresses. These characters have the least interest in pursuing money, power, fame, or physical pleasure; they are not perfect, but they know what courage and duty are, and have a fuller measure of virtue than most. If Plutarch is correct, it is in promoting virtue, in particular through characters such as these, that *Battlestar Galactica* is the most philosophical.

D. Marriage

So immorality in the new *Galactica* does not preclude its being morally beneficial and can even make it so—if we approach the story with discernment and think about it critically.

---

[44] "Pegasus," Season 2, Episode 10, directed by Michael Rymer and written by Anne Cofell Saunders; "Resurrection Ship: Part 1," Season 2, Episode 11, directed by Michael Rymer and written by Anne Cofell Saunders and Michael Rymer (Universal Television, 2006).

[45] The "Miniseries," Part 2.

[46] "Home: Parts 1 and 2," Season 2, episodes 6-7, Part 1 directed by Sergio Mimica-Gezzan and written by David Eick (Universal Television, 2005); Part 2 directed by Jeff Woolnough and written by David Eick and Ronald D. Moore (Universal Television, 2005).

[47] *Battlestar Galactica*, "Daybreak: Part 2," Season 4, Episode 22; directed by Michael Rymer and written by Ronald D. Moore (Universal Television, 2009).

Although the series explores numerous interesting ethical issues,[48] sexuality makes a particularly helpful case study in light of ancient reflections on virtue, which commonly focused on this topic. Marriage was very important to a number of ancient philosophers who saw it as the cure for the sexual dangers of youth.[49] In marriage sexuality does little if any harm and the most good; marriage turns sexual desire to the productive end of rearing children, thus placing it at the furthest remove from Baltar's raging lust. In promoting marriage the philosophers had some help from the poets: Homer eventually brings Odysseus home to his Penelope, and when Virgil's tale ends we know that Aeneas will marry Lavinia. Marriage doesn't come off quite as well in the new *Galactica*, but it could have been a lot worse. After looking at four examples, proceeding from the worst to the better, I shall summarize the problem of marriage in *Galactica* and comment on one aspect of *Galactica* which Plutarch's principles cannot redeem.

There is little more to say about our first example; for most of the series Gaius Baltar's lust runs wild, wreaking destruction on his life, his acquaintances (who, due to his behavior, are not genuine friends), and his entire world. It poisons everything he touches, making him unstable as well as unreliable and dangerous at his jobs: first as scientist, then as vice president, and later as president. This is sexual desire at its worst.

The lives of Kara and Lee are a good example of the dangers of sexual desire, but they also display a degree of restraint. Unlike Baltar, and with rare exception (Kara's past relationship with Zak), they don't allow their relationships to interfere with their duties. During the finale to Season 2 they both marry other people. Later we learn that the marriages were undertaken somewhat spontaneously after Kara and Lee slept together.[50] Each, at times, regrets their marriages. They are tempted to cheat, but do not; Kara, it seems, does not believe in divorce but is willing to commit adultery, while Lee has no problem with divorce but will not commit adultery. Returning to his wife, Lee confesses his conflicted feelings and recommits to her.[51] May I suggest that this episode in their lives illustrates that the best thing is to protect marriage as much as possible, to enter into it wisely, and to avoid both divorce *and* adultery.

This brings us to the Tyrol family. Some time after his affair with Sharon, Galen marries his old friend Cally. Their marriage lasts as long as they do, and we have encouraging evidence of them working through problems together.[52] After all the destruction wrought on society and on relationships by riotous sexual desire, it would be refreshing to see love turned to creative rather than destructive ends. For a time we are led to believe that in the context of Galen's marriage to Cally sexual desire has at last found a productive end, for the Tyrol family has a son, baby Nicholas; to all appearance the Tyrols are following the advice of ancient philosophers. Sadly, we soon learn that Nicholas was conceived during a relationship Cally had with someone

---

[48] Some of these issues include democracy, just warfare, weapons of mass destruction, suicide bombings, genocide, the torturing of terrorists, and the balancing of national security and civil rights. The reader interested in these issues will find some helpful analyses in *Battlestar Galactica and Philosophy: Knowledge Here Begins Out There*, published by Blackwell, as well as *Battlestar Galactica and Philosophy: Mission Accomplished or Mission Frakked Up?*, edited by Josef Steiff and Tristan D. Tamplin (Chicago: Open Court Press), 2008.

[49] To name a few philosophers who spoke highly of marriage: Plato in his *Laws*, Book VIII # 839a-b; Cicero in his *Treatise on the Chief Good and Evil*, Book IV, chapter 7, and Book V, chapter 23; and Augustine in his *Confessions*, Book II, chapter 2.

[50] *Battlestar Galactica*, "Unfinished Business," Season 3, Episode 13; directed by Robert Young and written by Michael Taylor (Universal Television, 2006).

[51] *Battlestar Galactica*, "The Eye of Jupiter," Season 3, Episode 11; directed by Michael Rymer and written by Mark Verheiden (Universal Television, 2006); "Taking a Break from All Your Worries," Season 3, Episode 13; directed by Edward James Olmos and written by Michael Taylor (Universal Television, 2007).

[52] *Battlestar Galactica*, "A Day in the Life," Season 3, Episode 15; directed by Rod Hardy and written by Mark Verheiden (Universal Television, 2007).

else shortly before she married Tyrol.[53] Although their marriage is a faithful one and lasts "till death does them part," Cally has deceived her husband about her son the whole time.

But there is one successful marriage, one which succeeds where the philosophers hoped. Karl and Athena Agathon's love produces a child, Hera. Their relationship, admittedly, does not *begin* in a good marriage, but with a passionate affair on Caprica.[54] Yet it ends up there just the same. Their love is marked by loyalty and fecundity; and when the story draws to a close, this, the purest example of love on the *Galactica*, is the best reason the survivors of the Human-Cylon war have to hope for a good future.

The makers of *Galactica* are reticent to portray a good marriage. At the end of the series any viewer is disappointed who hopes that Kara and Lee, each now single, will marry.[55] Meanwhile Adama has been a divorcee since the story began, and it is known that Colonel Tigh's wife Ellen sleeps around. Through all the failings of marriages on the *Galactica* one can descry the shining ideal of a good marriage; one gets the feeling that marriage is the best context for sexual love. One also gets the feeling that practically no one ever attains this ideal. Nevertheless, one does get the feeling that the ideal is worth fighting for, and that there is hope for a good, or at least a better, marriage. In the last episode the Tighs are reunited; the Agathons, on a peaceful planet at last, are beginning their new life raising Hera; and even Baltar has turned a new corner, apparently ready to settle down with his old partner, Caprica Six, and take up a living built on honest labor rather than his old habits of deception.[56]

A final note is in order concerning a problem in *Galactica* with which Plutarch cannot help us. The ancient philosophers can tell us little about the powerful new visual medium through which the *Galactica*'s tale is told. Television brings to life not just ideas but the images of sordid deeds. It was not always so with fiction; three lines after Vergil tells us that Dido and Aeneas met in a cave he describes the awful consequences of the affair, the terrible Carthaginian wars. We are given the details of the weather at the time, but no details about what happens in the cave.[57] In shocking contrast to Vergil, the reimagined *Battlestar Galactica* provides images of sexual misdeeds, some of them not too far removed from pornography. In this respect the new *Galactica* through its film medium is more dangerous than any fiction the ancient philosophers encountered in the older medium consisting of mere words.

IV. SAINT AUGUSTINE ON THE BATTLESTAR *GALACTICA*

Augustine's *The City of God* is known for its presentation of Augustine's philosophy of history and of his thinking on the relationship of the Church and society, not to mention as an example of early Christian apologetics. However, Book XIX of *The City of God* is significant for another reason, namely for developing a Christian perspective on the value of the arts. For here Augustine develops an argument that, when paired with *How a Young Man Should Study Poems*, extends Plutarch's philosophical defense of the arts in a theological direction. Like other Christian medieval thinkers, Augustine found much to appreciate in the pagan philosophers. The Platonists, Stoics, and even the Epicureans agreed on one principle Augustine found insightful:

---

53 *Battlestar Galactica*, "A Disquiet Follows My Soul," Season 4, Episode 14; directed and written by Ronald D. Moore (Universal Television, 2009).

54 *Battlestar Galactica*, "Six Degrees of Separation," Season 1, Episode 7; directed by Robert M. Young and written by Michael Angeli (Universal Television, 2005).

55 *Battlestar Galactica*, "Daybreak: Part 2."

56 Ibid.

57 Vergil, *Aeneid: Selections from Books 1, 2, 4, 6, 10, and 12*; 2d ed; ed. Barbara Weiden Boyd (Wauconda, IL: Bolchazy-Carducci Publishers, 2004); Book IV, lines 165-172.

A happy life requires virtue. We have seen that Plutarch supports this as well, and that his advice for partaking of fiction with discernment leads to confirmation of this principle from literature and, in our day, from film. But, for Augustine, this is not enough. No happy life in this world, in this life and in and through ourselves, is finally attainable—not even for the most virtuous—not for Socrates, Cicero, or Adama. This world we inhabit, and we who inhabit it, have been too wrecked by sin. Accordingly, happiness requires grace. Happiness is not found in this world, in ourselves, or by ourselves; it is found in God, who is not in but above us, and it is found by grace. The philosophical quest for happiness, in its failure, thus shows the need for a religious pursuit of happiness.[58] After summarizing Augustine's argument from Book XIX, I will show how *Galactica* illustrates his argument.

Augustine describes in Book XIX of *The City of God* "the reasonings by which men have attempted to make for themselves a happiness in this unhappy life."[59] Borrowing from Varro, he summarizes as many as 288 possible positions a philosopher could take on the happy life and how to obtain it. But, he says, Christians see things differently. To the views of the philosophers, Christians "reply that life eternal is the supreme good, death eternal the supreme evil, and that to obtain the one and escape the other we must live rightly."[60] But immediately Augustine, like the Apostle Paul before him, references Habakkuk 2:4, saying that we do not have "in ourselves power to live rightly," and so must pursue happiness with faith. The problem is that the philosophers have sought happiness "in this life and in themselves," when neither this life nor ourselves will suffice for happiness.

This life will not suffice for happiness: "For what flood of eloquence can suffice to detail the miseries of this life?"[61] Diseases, natural disasters, deaths of loved ones, and one's own inevitable death—there is just too much suffering in life to call it happy. Human society, in the peace of which the happy life would subsist if it were possible, is rife with misery.[62] The best of friendships and marriages have quarrels, and all nations undergo the trials of war. We long for peace in and among our societies and with each other.[63] But, even when we have it, peace is unstable; we cannot count on it to last.[64]

Ourselves will not suffice for happiness. Augustine points out that even virtue serves only "to wage perpetual war with vices," not the vices of others but *our own* vices.[65] He agrees with various ancient philosophers that "the very virtues of this life . . . are certainly its best and most useful possessions," but he also says that they are "all the more telling proofs" of the misery of life, which they help us to endure. Virtue "has not perfect authority over vice," and, "however well one maintains the conflict" against sin, inevitably sin invades our lives: "there steals in some evil thing," which sullies our words if not our deeds, and our thoughts if not our words.[66] The really, genuinely *good* human being does not exist, save Jesus Christ; even being *pretty good* comes at the cost of a constant and arduous struggle within ourselves.

Accordingly, we must seek happiness where it may be found, namely in God. In addition to practicing virtue as the pagan philosophers did, if a person wants happiness he must pursue it

58 The reader interested in this aspect of Augustine's thought would do well to consult Brian Harding's *Augustine and Roman Virtue* (New York: Continuum Books, 2008).

59 Augustine, *City of God*, trans. Marcus Dods, Book XIX, chapter 1.

60 Ibid., chapter 4.

61 Ibid.

62 Ibid., chapter 5.

63 Ibid., chapter 12.

64 Ibid., chapter 5.

65 Ibid., chapter 4.

66 Ibid., chapter 27.

through theological means. He must submit himself to God; "beg from God grace to do his duty, and the pardon of sins;" "render to God thanks for all the blessings he receives;" and look forward to an eternal life which includes but perfects such happiness as this one allows, with no amount of misery mixed in.[67]

The characters on *Galactica* have ample reason to believe that happiness "in this life and in themselves" is not possible. They have witnessed uncountable deaths, their world has been consumed by war, and their interpersonal relationships are chaotic and turbulent. While the relatively virtuous do relatively well, none are fully happy, and all struggle with vice and temptations. A few examples from the (mostly) happy ending of *Galactica*, where human and Cylon survivors have found a new world on which to live peacefully, should suffice. Galen Tyrol is so hurt by recent events that he gives up on society altogether and resolves to dwell as a hermit someplace cold.[68] Roslin and Adama, now lovers, also abandon society, spending a short time together before Roslin dies of cancer. After burying her, Adama apparently finishes his days alone, talking out loud to her memory. Karl and Athena Agathon apparently live out a good life together, and Hera may have considered herself happy. It is revealed that the planet they are on is prehistoric Earth and that Hera is the ancestor of our own human race, the mother of all its achievements and joys. But she is also the mother of the collective misery of our planet's troubled history; if Augustine's analysis of human life is correct, the misery coming from Hera far outweighs her happiness.

Indeed, *Galactica*'s conclusion produces a glimmer of theological hope. Baltar's conversion to a better way of life is instigated by his newfound religious commitments.[69] Kara has apparently died and resurrected bodily; she mysteriously disappears, leaving behind her memory as a testimony to the other survivors of the hope of some manner of life after death. It is revealed that there are benevolent higher powers in the universe. They are not almighty; some are the sort of beings we might call "gods" or "angels," and they work for someone who doesn't like to be called "God."[70] So *Galactica*'s religion is far from Augustine's orthodox Christianity. Nevertheless, the characters' need for religious hope illustrates his point: Since we want to be happy and cannot do it in this life and by ourselves, we need divine help from beyond ourselves. In sum, modern fiction, even when focusing on deeply flawed characters, can still be of spiritual benefit, showing the insight of the ancient philosophers that virtue matters; the state of one's soul matters. But in doing so, science fiction also confirms the insight of ancient theologians, for it shows what ancient philosophy showed in its noble but unsuccessful attempt to obtain happiness in this life: that it cannot be done. We cannot reach happiness, not least because we cannot reach virtue. So we need God.[71]

V. CONCLUSION

We must handle fiction with care. We must be particularly cautious with a show like the reimagined *Battlestar Galactica*, which vividly portrays a world that is mixed with good and evil

---

67 Ibid.

68 *Battlestar Galactica*, "Daybreak: Part 2." Galen's chosen home may be Scotland, since he mentions "highlands."

69 Baltar's conversion is extremely interesting and deserves a fuller analysis. Unfortunately, such an analysis would necessarily be lengthy and, it seems to me, would require a close look at thinkers other than Augustine and Plutarch. I hope to investigate Baltar's conversion in more detail at a later time. For our present purposes, we need only note that it hints at our need for grace.

70 "Daybreak: Part 2."

71 The astute reader will notice that this is an argument that, *if* we are going to be happy, we need virtue and grace—not that we can actually *be* happy. Such an argument would require an additional argument that a gracious God exists; this is only an argument that we have *a need* for such a God.

and populated by imperfect creatures. This is not a show for children; only the most careless parents would want their children's worldview shaped by the moral ambiguity and their views on love shaped by the sex-soaked culture of the human-Cylon war. That does not mean we cannot derive some benefit from it. It may be true that *Galactica* classic, in its moral clarity, would pass Socrates' standards for acceptable fiction in the *Republic*. However, if Plutarch and Augustine are right, then the reimagined *Galactia* has this advantage over the original: It describes a world more like our own, and characters more like us. We must only enter into the world of *Battlestar Galactica*, and the worlds of similar contemporary fiction, armed with caution and discernment, lest we be allured by the wrong things or misunderstand the right things. Rightly interpreting fiction such as this is a task for mature interpreters whose moral outlook is already well formed, and it is an important task. Plutarch's remark is worth paraphrasing. We cannot prevent people from watching shows like *Battlestar Galactica*; perhaps we wouldn't want to if we could. Instead, let us learn how to watch such shows with discernment, and teach others to do the same. When we watch with discernment, we learn not only the lesson of the ancient philosophers that a happy life requires virtue, but also the lesson of ancient theologians that a happy life requires grace. Modern fiction, even of the very sordid variety, shows what ancient philosophy shows; but, according to Augustine, ancient philosophy shows our need for grace; so modern fiction also shows our need for grace.

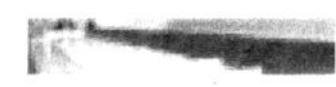

Magic, Muggles and Misunderstanding: A Conversation with Leigh Hickman About the Christ-like Wizard that Christian Culture Mistook for the Devil

by **Kevin C. Neece**

Leigh Hickman is an accomplished Christian scholar and an adjunct professor of English at Dallas Baptist University, as well as an editor for this publication. She is also devoted to studying popular works like *Jesus Christ Superstar*, the *Twilight* saga and *Wicked*, works that often seem to court theological controversy or feature vampires, monsters or magic. She sees in their popularity an indication of deep longings in the human heart—specifically, a longing for Christ. Most notably, Hickman has a particular affinity for and expertise in the *Harry Potter* books and films. Reflecting more than a decade of intense, careful study of, as she terms it, "all things Harry," she was kind enough to share with me the discoveries she has made within the *Potter* text—discoveries, she says, of the story of Christ embedded in "one of the central narratives of our time."

Hickman began researching the *Harry Potter* series in 2001 and has since collected "virtually every book in print" as well as every academic paper and article she can find on the subject, especially as reflects a Christian perspective. Though fears that the novels would lead young readers away from the gospel and into occultism caused much hand wringing and consternation in Christian culture—from the press and pulpits—Hickman was drawn to the book series because she arrived at an entirely different assessment. "I knew instinctively," she says, "that if there is a cultural phenomenon, [Christ] is going to be at the heart of it somewhere, bringing glory to himself. I knew that this was worthy of a good conversation and I wanted to be as well-versed as possible on it." Though the study of *Harry Potter* is a scholarly pursuit for Hickman, it is born of a deep love for the books themselves and for the gospel she sees clearly and even intentionally reflected in their pages. "I do it because I love the story," she tells me, "I'm a fan first and foremost."

Given the amount of vociferous criticism that has been leveled against *Harry Potter* in Christian circles for nearly two decades, one might expect Hickman to be alone in her quest. Not so, she responds, citing such works as *The Gospel According to Harry Potter* by Connie Neal and John Granger's *Looking for God in Harry Potter*, which she says "blew my head off" by more deeply opening a positive Christian reading of the books. "Overwhelmingly," Hickman tells me, "I have read more Christian scholarship about *Harry Potter* affirming its merit than vilifying it. The people that do vilify it, however, get the most press."

These critics, Hickman is convinced, represent "a very small minority who have a very large megaphone." In her experience, the complaints coming from this loud minority have sprung largely from ignorance. "99.999% of the people who have a problem with it," she tells me, "haven't cracked a page. I've never known anyone who was against *Harry Potter* who had read the book." As Hickman sees it, the real problem is a "dualism and anti-intellectualism" in Christian culture, which assumes that "someone else needs to do your thinking for you" and has spawned mass avoidance of *Potter* among Christians.

When asked why such vitriol has arisen against the series, Hickman replies, "My first instinct is that we're very concerned about false Christs and that we're very concerned about false prophets. It's an old-time fear that some false god will displace the authority of Christ." But this view is rooted, she says, "in a fundamental distrust of the Holy Spirit's work in another's life and a fundamental distrust of God. The people who are most afraid of *Harry Potter*, in my opinion, are the people whose God isn't very big. If J.K. Rowling can overthrow Jesus Christ, then Jesus Christ isn't all that powerful." Because of this, she says, the popular Christian campaigns against the *Potter* books and films are "symptoms of the very thing they claim to treat – which is a lack of discernment. They are manifestations of a lack of discernment in the Church."

It is for this reason that Hickman feels there is still much work to be done in recasting this conversation within Christian culture. "J.K. Rowling," she explains, "has gift-wrapped this for Christian culture to discuss." In fact, she says, the hostility leveled toward *Potter* by Christians does more than miss an obvious opportunity; it amounts to a failure to fulfill the cultural mandate of the Church. "When Christian culture abandons one of the primary narratives of our time, that's not well-disciplined stewardship of Creation. If it is capturing the hearts and minds of our generation, then [by not discussing it] we're losing a great opportunity to enchant hearts and minds for Christ."

When it comes to researching a topic as deeply as she has *Harry Potter*, Hickman says, "I think that's always my primary motivation—whether I can better see what I love the most through it." And see it she has—not just in the series' ultimate conclusion, where even mainstream journalists noted the Christ imagery, but from the first time she picked up *Harry Potter and the Sorcerer's Stone* and read of the titular hero as an orphaned baby being placed on his relatives' doorstep. "From chapter one, Harry's dropped off at the Dursley's and doesn't know how special he is. He doesn't know that he's the chosen one. You've got this child out in the elements in the cold, dark night who's come to inhabit this place. And he's incredibly special and yet [living] in the limitations of the normal and the everyday. It was so beautiful that I actually teared up. Literally, I have a note in the margin of my book: 'Insert manger scene here.'"

The Christ imagery in the books is far more than circumstantial. J.K. Rowling, the now internationally famous author of the *Potter* book series, is a self-described Christian whose narrative is laced with far more than incidental Scriptural themes and images of Christ. As Hickman explored the books more deeply, "it just became more and more apparent that this is no accident. And that was what was really exciting to me because I knew that the reasons I was invested in the book had everything to do with this Christocentric through-line in the book. But, when I found out that it was quite possibly intentional, that's what made me really excited." In fact, Rowling herself confirmed as early as 2007, after the release of the final book in the series, that there had always been deep Christian themes in the books and that the titular wizard was always intended to be a Christ figure.[1]

"Harry lives with great purpose," Hickman says, "with great sacrificial purpose. And I think that is one of the keys to his success and the keys to people's affection for him. He lives out of a purpose and out of a heartbeat of sacrifice that is so needed and so foreign and people vicariously enjoy his certainty about how he loves other people and how he lays down his life for other people. And they enjoy that because they're designed and created to engage in that story and to do that for other people." In the passionate following of the *Harry Potter* books and films, Hickman sees people who are drawn to something that reflects the God they were made to worship.

"If I've learned anything about the cultural phenomenon that surrounds Harry Potter," she tells me, "it's that people—this is very simple—people want to worship Jesus Christ." It's a universal desire, she says, that is deep in the human heart. "People are attracted to him. People

---

1 Shawn Adler, "'Harry Potter' Author J.K. Rowling Opens Up About Books' Christian Imagery," MTV News, October 17, 2007, http://www.mtv.com/news/articles/1572107/jk-rowling-talks-about-christian-imagery.jhtml

like the way he smells; people like the way he tastes. People want to worship him." And, in her view, it is the way in which people see Christ reflected in the *Harry Potter* books and films that, whether they realize it or not, draws them so strongly to the story and to its eponymous central character. "It's about a young man's journey to give his life away. That's what the story is. Harry continually, from book one to book seven, always makes the choice—in battle with another will inside him that doesn't want to do it—to give his life away for other people. And in doing that, he always wins, after going through the crucible of great human suffering and loss."

According to Hickman, Harry's Christ-like role is no one-time metaphor in the story. He is a savior in every book in the series. "He is continually bringing people out from the dead," Hickman says. "He is bringing people back from the dead. He is [rescuing] things that are particularly stolen away by demonic, Satanic images like snakes...He takes people away, literally, from snakes and dragons. ... He snatches people, literally, from the flame that they will die in unless he grabs hold of them and throws them up behind him." She stops for a moment, remarking, "Behind him, not in front of him. It's important. If you want to live, you get behind this guy. You join his ranks. You let him teach you."

It would seem, then, that one of the Christian community's loudest protests over a popular work of art was set squarely against a book series by a Christian author whose globally adored hero is one of the most widely read Christ figures in recent history. It's no wonder that Hickman refers to Jesus' acts of opening the ears of the deaf and the eyes of the blind as a metaphor for the Church's need to open its eyes and ears to the heart of God reflected in the popular voices of our culture. "We are the people who claim to see," she says, "and yet we are blind."

Hickman does not believe, however, that Rowling's intent with her books was purely evangelistic. "I think she's writing the world that she would like to see. I think she is writing the hero that she wants to believe in. I sincerely feel more angst in her answers than I do when I read C.S. Lewis or even Tolkien. And that, to me, is one of the greatest appeals of Harry Potter. She lets him suffer. She lets him question and she lets him doubt and that is the greatest service she can give to her modern readers. And to me, that is a precious thing. It's hands reaching through the dark to find God."

Like the father of the possessed boy in the Gospel of Mark who said, "I believe; help my unbelief," Hickman sees Rowling confessing faith, even as she admits the struggle that faith involves. "I sense her saying, 'I'm writing this in trust that it's true.' It's a beautiful, beautiful thing. I do not believe she wrote this as a witnessing tool. I don't believe she wrote this to necessarily evangelize." But, she says, "I think it *is* a witnessing tool and it does evangelize my heart...big time. But it does so precisely because it meets me where I am, in my doubts, in my uncertainties, in my fears, in my unspoken angst that I hope this is real. And, in that way, it's unlike any fantasy novel that I've ever read. Precisely because of that."

Hickman sees great opportunities for positive Christian dialogue in the breadth of popular artistic expressions available to us, suggesting that a renewed perspective might allow Christians to follow their innate interests into greater engagement with their culture. "There are so few workers in this field, and yet there is so much to glean out of it," she says. "You don't need to look at thirty different narratives. Just look at the ones that matter. Some Christians are called to certain narratives because God speaks uniquely to them through that story." She encourages others to find what draws them and "glean in that field, because more than likely, the reason that your affections are in that field is because you need to speak to people who are in that field with you who love it. You're uniquely called to speak to those people. … Share Christ through what has grabbed your heart and your affections."

Hickman hopes that sharing her discoveries of the gospel reflected in the *Harry Potter* books and films will help draw others to a deeper love for and understanding of Christ. She also hopes it will encourage Christians to see God at work in their culture and to act as interpreters for those around them. Every Christian, she says, is called to speak to their culture in some way and she hopes to encourage a deeper conversation of the influential narratives of our time. "The workers are few and the time is really limited," she says, "Come on. Come on."

For more information on Leigh Hickman or to book her as a speaker, please email her at profleigh7@gmail.com.

This piece is adapted from works previously published in *New Identity Magazine* and on the Art House Dallas blog.

Visual Art

Dawn Waters Baker

www.dawnwatersbaker.com
www.dawnsartsite.blogspot.com

ARTIST STATEMENT:

> "Blessed are the men of Noah's race that build
> their little arks, though frail and poorly filled,
> and steer through winds contrary towards a wraith,
> a rumour of a harbour guessed by faith."
> --From Tolkien in his work,Tree and Leaf

I like to think of my work as striving towards that harbour: painting the delicate light with a still hush as through a clouded pane of glass. It's almost as if you have walked into an enchanted place where the trees and sky can talk, where everything is a metaphor of our gritty world. Only, here, it has been given a softness of light, a feeling, a glimpse into the mystery.

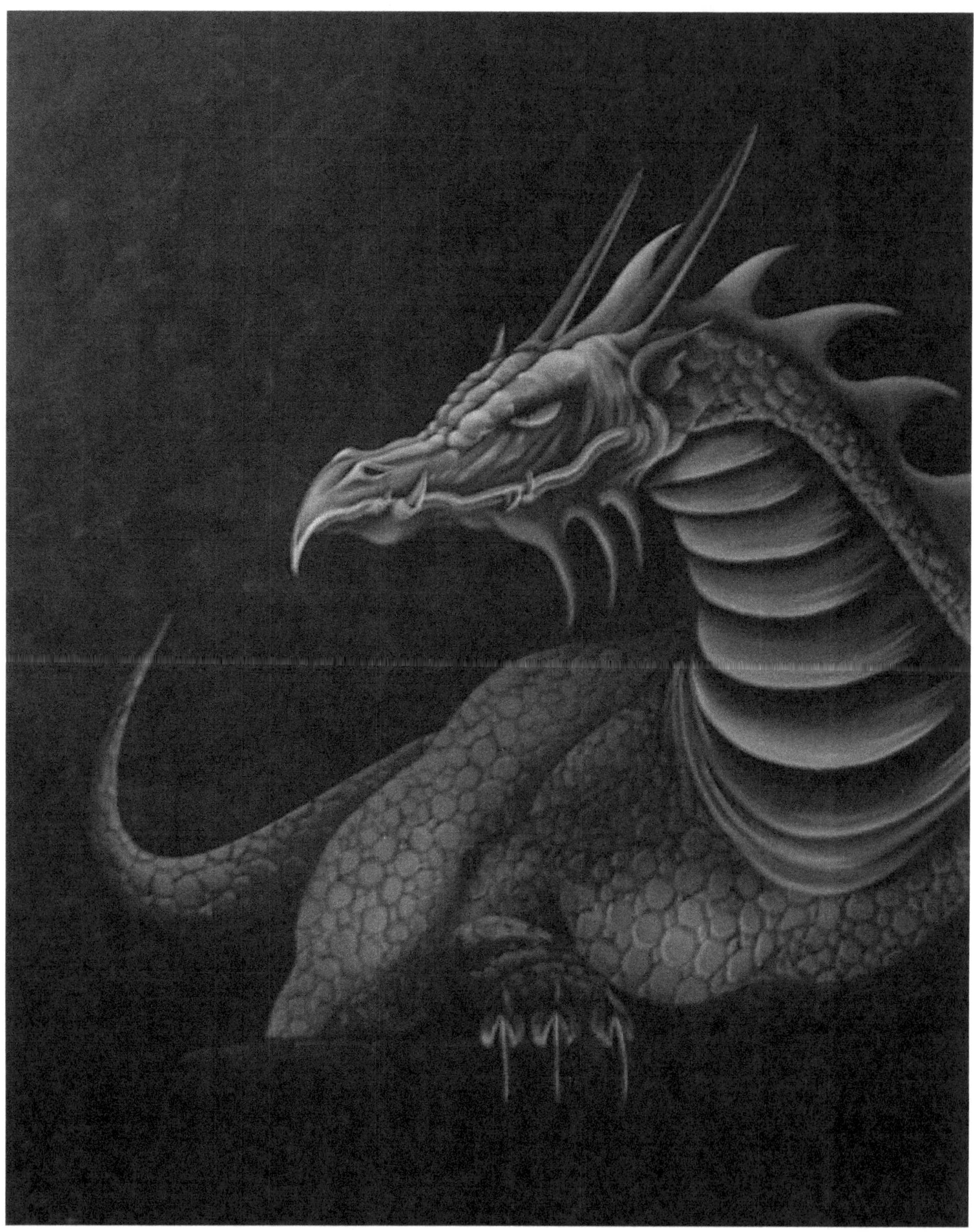

Lust

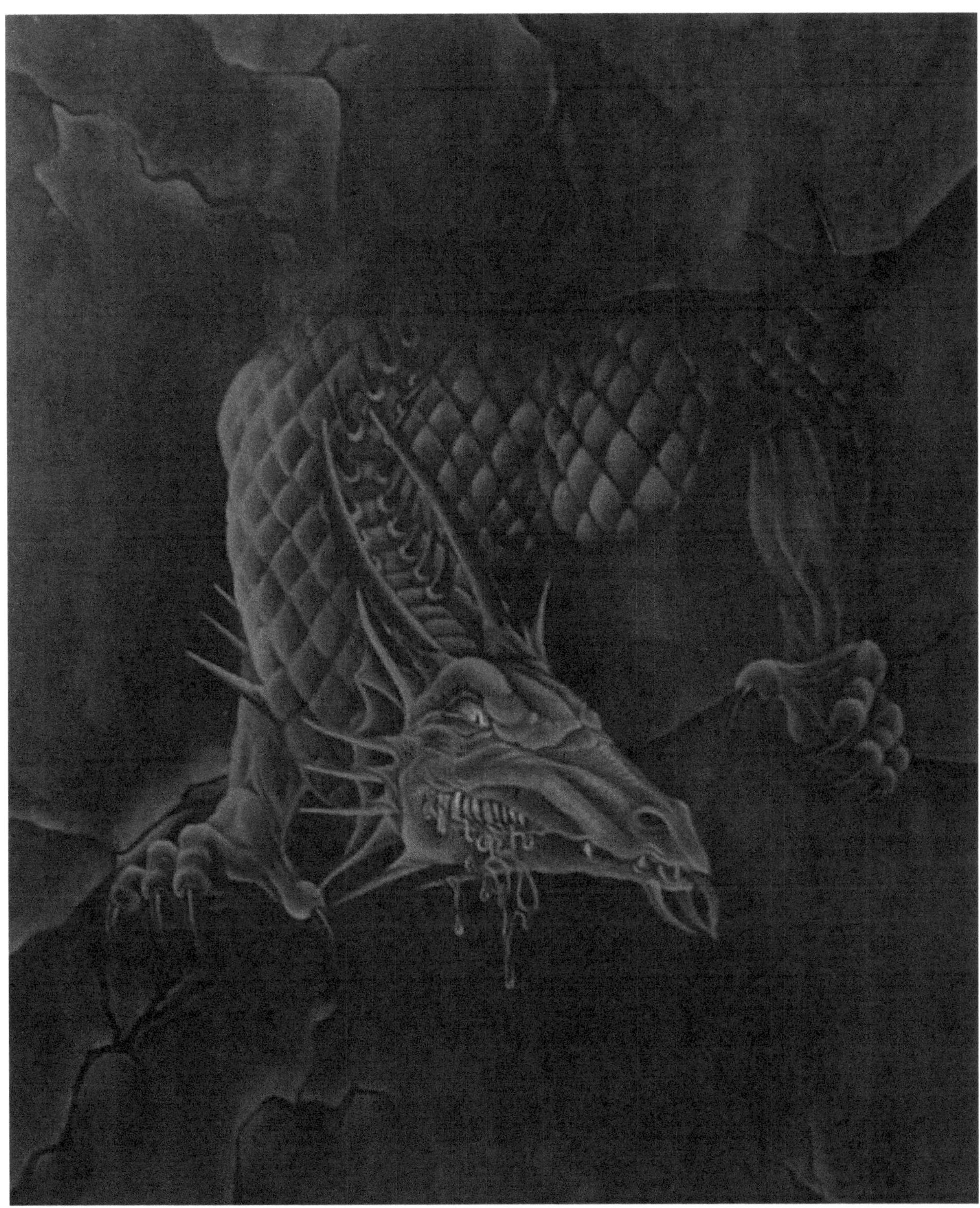

Violence

Poetry

Caitlin Smith

How to…

Wait 'till the day is mysty magical
    And stars glint in the solstice light;
Walk alone in the dark dancing woods;
    Amble through the open prairie;
When you see the ring
    Halt!
Time moves strangely here.

Take a step.
Toe carefully into the ring,
Take care not to muss the grass,
Trip a stone, or crush a
Toadstool.
They did dance here
    Some seconds ago.
Turn slowly—windershins of course,
    Seconds stop and hours race along.
Some one—thing—will take your hand,
Step with it, into Their land.

The wind will catch in your hair
    And the stars shine brighter here in
This underground world.
    A hall will dazzle your senses.
Look—and see all your eyes can taste,
    Hear the music that haunts and frenzies…
Lilting waterfalls, pipes, drums, storms, and spring
    Don't Dance!
Time twists strangely here.

They will dazzle you with
Their brilliant smiles and
The way They move through air,
The beat pulling Them along.
    See those like me and like you
Who caught the rhythm, to never be free
    Blink!
Time stops for no mouse.

Do not touch the drink
        Sparkling ambrosia that Midas could not scorn.
Do not! taste the fare
        Sweet tarts and dainty bits will hold you
        Stronger than iron.

But what wonders that hold underground
        Shubert and Mozart collaborate in a corner while
Behind poets declaim and
        Star-bound Van Gogh paints
Those taken by the Muse.

Remember the world from whence you come
        Of love and warmth, war and fire,
Remind yourself of trees and streams and home
        Of a mother's lullaby, sweet and tame
Recall what Time is…

Close your eyes again.
Turn against the windershins.
And step.

When you return to the world, they will have been looking
        A day
                A month
                        A year
They thought you lost.
        Taken
Not gone of your own accord.
You will not correct them
Nor remember all yourself.
Time moves differently here.
It will be forgotten
        In a year
                A month
                        A day.

No one will understand.
        But you.
                And me.
                        And those others in between.
That there is a gleam in the velvet night
        And a sparkling darkness within the dew.
That there is a place where Time bends to
        Another force—a wilder dance.

You know
And I know
And others in between
Of a place of danger, peril, and desire
And a time that moves strangely here.

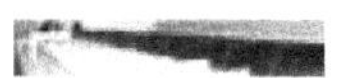

Creative Writing

An Interview with Dr. Zaius

Daniel J. Heisey

Over a recent holiday break from my academic work, I once again booked an excursion to Central City on the planet Soror. On this occasion I managed to arrange, through contacts developed over the years, a meeting with that most eminent scholar, Dr. Zaius, Minister of Science and Chief Defender of the Faith. We met in his austere yet dignified office in the Natural History Museum, and I found him much as he is described in the chronicle by Pierre Boulle: "He was shorter than the gorillas and slightly round-shouldered. His arms were relatively longer so that he often touched the ground with his hands as he walked, which the other apes did only rarely . . . . His head adorned with long coarse hair and sunk between his shoulders, his face frozen in an expression of pedantic meditation, he looked like a venerable and solemn old pontiff." Although at the time of M. Boulle's narrative Dr. Zaius wore a black frock coat and grey striped trousers reminiscent of the formal apparel of a gentleman from our Edwardian era, when I encountered him he was splendidly attired in the familiar burnished orange suit of more recent vintage, draped with a matching stole embellished with significant glyphs to convey his learned and holy status. After formal greetings of a cordial nature, I began:

I see that you are a collector of antiquarian books.

One must know the past. As I told General Urko many years ago, "No information is useless." I still stand by that truth. As I get older, I find antiquarian study of more and more fascination. It teaches so many lessons.

Which books would you take with you to the proverbial desert island?

One of my favorites of these old books is called *Meditations*, by Marcus Aurelius, a very simian name, you cannot deny. In fact, my secretary is named Aurelius, a very capable young ape, even though he's a chimpanzee. As I was saying, though, that wise old ape, Marcus Aurelius, wrote that, "The first rule is to keep an untroubled spirit. The second is to look things in the face and know them for what they are." Noble words, worthy of an ape. It's my privilege to occupy a position where I can do just that. The more I learn and the older I get, I sometimes wish I could go back in time and understand and even revise various chapters and scenes in my own life, but, as Marcus Aurelius teaches us, we must bravely face facts and carry on.

Perhaps along the lines of such revision, this critique from a colleague may be a propos. Dr. Zira once described you orangutans in this way: "They are Official Science. . . . They learn an enormous amount from books. They are all decorated. Some of them are looked upon as leading lights in a narrow specialized field that requires a good memory. Apart from that," and then she made a gesture of contempt. Strong words. How do you respond?

One of these old books, *On the Holy Spirit*, about that same Spirit who guided, I believe, our venerated Lawgiver, is by another wise old ape, named Basil, from somewhere called Cappadocia. I have a picture of it in another old book, and of all the places on your world, it's the only one I have seen that looks at all civilized. It has admirable dwellings carved into beautiful khaki colored rock cliffs. That wonderful place, so much like our own city here, is proof that this Basil was an ape, no doubt an orangutan, for who else would devise such brilliant structures and write what he wrote?

Yes, it's true that those man-made cave dwellings in southern Turkey do look a lot like your sort of large ant-hill structures built into the hillside here.

Right. Well, I refer to these words of Basil, the great troglodyte ape of Cappadocia: "Reverence for the mysteries is best encouraged by silence." And, as you have read in M. Boulle's account, and here for once he's reliable and accurate, "Meanwhile, the apes are meditating in silence. Their brain is developing in solitary reflection." Dr. Zira is a psychologist, albeit for animals, but she should know that Urko and Ursus and the other gorillas, for example, are extroverts, basically insecure and thus given to rash and impulsive action, often bullying and domineering, so I make no apologies for those of us who by our inner nature are drawn to lives of silence and seclusion, to live more deliberate, meditative lives, yet all the while putting to public use our skill for organization and edifying others by our scholarly writings.

In addition to being "official science," you orangutans have been described in these terms: "Pompous, solemn, pedantic, devoid of originality and critical sense, intent on preserving tradition, blind and deaf to all innovation, they form the substratum of every academy. Endowed with a good memory, they learn an enormous amount by heart and from books. Then they themselves write other books, in which they repeat what they have read, thereby earning the respect of their fellow orangutans. . . . Almost every orangutan has behind him a gorilla or a council of gorillas who support him and maintain him in an honorable post, seeing to it that he is granted the titles and decorations that are dear to his heart."

That is the biased caricature of Ulysse Mérou, a trained human protégé of Dr. Zira and, to an extent, of Dr. Cornelius. You're relying too much on the slanted, often satiric perspective of M. Boulle. I refuse to dignify that portrayal with a response, except to say to you: You are an academic. Do you not recognize yourself in that description?

Um, pass. But what about that term, "official science"? How can science be official?

First, let's understand what we mean by "science." Let's take a more capacious view, encompassing more than, for example, what we find in our Institute for Advanced Biological Study, and see "science" as a disciplined, systematic approach to knowledge, a discussion of what we know, that discussion being based on structured, rational arguments. Thus, when studying the past, we can take a scientific approach, debating the implications of facts, whether they're found in the ground or in a document.

What about those areas of knowledge where the facts are less concrete? Who's to say that Marcus Aurelius, for example, was noble, or that Basil was wise?

The same principle applies. So, likewise, when studying transcendent, eternal being, and here I have in mind what we may call theology, we can also take a scientific approach, arguing in a rational, structured way from what we can observe and from what has been revealed. For example, how can we know what is just or ethical behavior? How can we know who's noble and wise, who's a scoundrel or an imbecile? It must be more than what any one particular individual feels at any given moment. That approach leaves too much to chance; low blood sugar, for example, or immaturity, not to mention not having all the facts. Besides, it's absurd to think that any one individual can determine what is always and everywhere true or virtuous. Thereby far too much is expected of one mind. Logical errors can have terrible consequences for all parties concerned, as well as for ages to come. So, you see, I and my colleagues, such as Dr. Maximus, must take a long view, seeing not only what's gone before, but also what could develop down the road. We are not being arbitrary but serving as stewards of the wisdom handed down from ages and ages of apes who have gone before us. Our Sacred Scrolls provide us with invaluable insights, and here apes such as Marcus Aurelius or Basil can tell us more than Dr. Zira or Dr. Cornelius.

You once had Dr. Zira and Dr. Cornelius indicted for "scientific heresy," but, as Dr. Zira herself had asked at the time, "How can scientific truth be heresy?"

In your world, do you not have such entities as *The New York Times* and the Académie française? They serve as guardians for established scholars, and woe to any young, or not so young, scholar who advances a theory or interpretation outside the accepted world view. From what I have seen, in your world someone, especially an academic, challenging the prevailing opinion of the intellectual community is ostracized, paraded through the public media and mocked, vilified, demonized.

It could be you're taking too narrow a sample for the basis of that characterization.

It would seem to me that there is no one more narrow, rigid, or authoritarian than one of your intellectuals, who all the while prides himself (or herself, as the case may be) on being fair and broad-minded. They appear, to this outsider, at any rate, to be tolerant of anyone who agrees with them. At least we had a hearing, at the highest level, free from media hysteria. Yet, as I told those young apes charged with heresy, "What I do, I do with no pleasure."

I notice on each visit, year after year, that humans are accorded better treatment, but they still do not have the right to vote. You once famously declared that, "Man has no understanding. He can be taught a few simple tricks, nothing more. . . . Man is a nuisance. He eats up his food supplies in the forest, then migrates to our green belts and ravages our crops. The sooner he is exterminated, the better." Later, you said, "From the evidence, I believe his wisdom must walk hand in hand with his idiocy. His emotions must rule his brain. He must be a warlike creature who gives battle to everything around him, even himself."

For the most part, those words, too, I still stand by. We have learned that exterminating man is impossible, even when it looks as though he will make himself extinct. We have found that to a degree, man can be domesticated. Thus the developing co-existence you have noticed. Nevertheless, voting requires reasoned discourse, and humans, with all due respect, are incapable of sustained rational thought.

I'll admit that one could point to certain evidence to support your case.

Of course! Why, can you imagine them taking part in our deliberations in the amphitheatre here? In the course of my long life, I have seen many of you visiting humans, from Ulysse Mérou to George Taylor to Alan Virdon and Peter Burke, and all were belligerent and devious, utterly unfit for responsible leadership in this society. We've learned to welcome tourists such as your good self, and you are indeed welcome to enjoy our cuisine and buy our post cards, but as for the permanent human residents here, there can be no further development.

Some would see your comments as patronizing and patriarchal.

I would suggest they need to expand their scope. My mandate is to safeguard the spiritual and intellectual patrimony of every ape, and the sad fact is, ultimately, human nature never changes, all schemes at perfection, whether by education or eugenics, notwithstanding. Until someone can convince me otherwise, I see no reason to change my mind.

You have held positions on the tribunal of the National Academy and on the High Council, but what does the future have in store for you?

As I study the past, I know that eternity awaits us all. In the Sacred Scrolls there are various literary genres, not only historical accounts and laws from our great Lawgiver, but also poetry. One such poem that has long sustained me concludes with these words: "And when I die, His loving care/Will raise me from the sod/To learn the perfect Mischief there,/The Nimbleness of God."

With respect, Your Excellency, I believe those lines are from a poem entitled, "The Theology of Bongwi, the Baboon," by a twentieth-century British poet, Roy Campbell.

If I may, that's a typical human delusion, to assume that all that's true, good, and beautiful comes from humans. That is indeed the title of the poem, but the very name Bongwi, and the fact that it records the wisdom of a baboon, a line all but extinct now, proves its antiquity.

Do you see any contradiction between being Minister of Science and Chief Defender of the Faith? I mean, even though you say you believe that "no information is useless," you once ordered the demolition of an archaeological site, and you ordered the destruction of computer files found in the ruins of an abandoned human city.

There is no contradiction between faith and reason. To put them in opposition to one another is an error, one only a human could make. The two positions I occupy are in complete harmony with one another, since both use complementary facets of the intellect and the memory. That being said, that ruined city you call "abandoned" was so because it had been destroyed, and that violent end came not from apes, but from man. My scientific studies, my antiquarian and archaeological interests, have informed my faith as it has been revealed to us in the Sacred Scrolls, namely, that man is a menace to himself and to others, that he carries within himself the infection of destruction.

But man is also capable of great good. After all, cities such as the one you refer to prove that humans can achieve elaborate levels of civilization.

Man's history shows example after example that given enough time, he uses, rather, misuses science for devastation and annihilation; he separates science from faith and turns a paradise into a desert. Man could not see, such are the limitations of his brain, that science by itself is a monster unleashed. We see that peril, as well as the problem of faith going all woolly from lack of clear and critical thinking. Perhaps over the years I have erred on the side of caution and have sought to monitor various data, but you'll admit, I bear grave responsibility for our social order. I believe I've acted with prudence, to prevent my civilization from suffering the same fate as the human one that went before. As I said long ago, and will say again and again, as many times as necessary, "It's a question of simian survival."

Fair enough, I suppose, but as you "bravely face facts and carry on," how would you now address a conflict between an article of faith and a scientific discovery?

Truth cannot contradict truth. It's an axiomatic principle. The conflict is when a scientific theory is doggedly, even dogmatically, asserted and defended as truth. Both science and religion have their orthodoxies, that I'll grant you, but the ultimate truth they seek is one, not two freakishly separate entities on different planets, so to speak. No doubt you have in mind the provocative new theory advanced by Dr. Cornelius that apes descended from man. He has shown me various fossils and fragments, and arraying them in a hypothetical "great chain of being," he convinces himself that there is an obvious and incontestable connection between one and another. As I once advised him, "Do not speak to me in absolutes. The evidence *is* contestable." It may be the grandest paradox: Faith makes us agnostic; there are some things we simply cannot know. Perhaps over millions of years apes have evolved, but that idea in no way puts paid to the belief that ape was created by God and endowed with a rational soul.

*

Suddenly a young chimpanzee appeared and stood discreetly a few paces from the curved desk; I had not heard the door open. Our hour together had gone by, and the interview was over. Dr. Zaius got up and came around the desk to me; looking up at me, he extended his long right arm and put his paw on my bowed head, imparting his blessing for my safe travels. He instructed the young chimpanzee, his secretary, Aurelius, to give me an official photograph, and then the great ape himself pressed into my hand a coupon for a free coffee and brioche at the museum's cafeteria.[1]

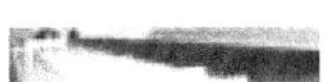

[1] For further reading: Pierre Boulle, *Planet of the Apes*, trans, Xan Fielding (New York: Signet, 1964); Marcus Aurelius, *Meditations*, trans. Maxwell Staniforth (Harmondsworth, UK: Penguin Books, 1964); Basil the Great, *On the Holy Spirit*, trans. David Anderson (Crestwood, NY: Saint Vladimir's Seminary Press, 1980); *The Collected Poems of Roy Campbell* (London: The Bodley Head, 1949). See also: *Planet of the Apes*, theatrical film (1968); *Planet of the Apes*, television series (1974); both available on DVD.

News from the Underground: Being an Unauthorized Account of Her Majesty's Secret Service

Jaclyn Young

The Players (in no particular order):

-Agent Elaine Barnesworthe—Field agent in the Secret Service of Her Majesty the Queen, whose origins remain as nebulous as her ability to control her temper under duress.

-Agent Ronald Justinian—Agent Barnesworthe's intrepid and idealistic half-Italian partner, prone to feats of daring, fits of melancholy, moments of epiphany, and the rescuing of damsels both in and out of distress.

-Capt. Gregory Cook—Commander of Her Majesty's Airship the Batista, fond of Queen and country, justice, duty, victory, duty, medals, speeches, duty, long ceremonies, and Earl Grey tea in the late afternoon, preferably with two sugars.

-Herr Dr. Schwarzbrennen—Mad (German) scientist, obsessed with black trench coats, platinum-blonde fauxhawks, shaded monocles, pyromania, anarchy, and world domination, sometimes even in that order.

-Jack Jeune—The mysterious writer of these tales, who might be female, might have been born in London and raised on the Continent, might be half French, might be on the run from both Queen Victoria and Dr. Schwarzbrennen, might have a mortal fear of ambiguity, and might be hiding in the basement of your home at this very moment. Then again, he (or she) might not. Her (or his) name might also mean "Young" in French. There's really no way to tell.

~ ~ ~ ~ ~ ~ ~

All characters appearing in this work are analogous. Any resemblance to real persons, evil or dead, is purely intentional.

Episode One:
Salvaged from the Ruins of a Smoldering Airship
(whose destruction could not possibly have been prevented by the author)

"A pretty little bluestocking[1] like your good self oughtn't be dashing about with sharp objects and explosive matter—you ought to be embroidering lace in some gilded mansion, with a gaggle of golden-haired brats flocked about you, conjugating Latin and quoting Shakespeare to their heart's content."

Agent Justinian was being difficult again, as was characteristic of his behavior when brandy and *Molto Sinistra* cigars became a significant factor in the social equation. Agent Barnesworthe continued polishing the firing mechanism of her uncocked aether-rifle without even gracing Just's comments with a weary sigh. His male chauvinism had very nearly given her an ulcer in the early days of their partnership, until Just had made the patent mistake of shattering the jaw of a Whitechapel bartender who had vociferously referred to her as, and I quote, "a gabby tart what just needs a good shagging." Ronald Justinian had only the highest estimation of Elaine Barnesworthe's character and capabilities, try as he might to hide that fact from her. His insults were a mere sham, and perhaps even an awkwardly endearing attempt at affection—

"I mean, good Lord, woman, how long do you expect me to keep your dear little ringlets from being singed off by some sun-mad anarchist Dago[2], eh?"

—a terribly misguided attempt at affection, then. Barnesworthe's fingers tightened on the aether-rifle and her eyes turned the shade of cerulean absinthe. For a moment she glared through her lashes at Justinian and seriously contemplated reminding him that his Italian mother's contribution to his heritage technically made him a "Dago." That being a blow far too below the belt (and consequently better saved for emergencies), she simply stretched her fashionably thin lips into a vampiric smile and said, "Are you aware of the modern term for gentlemen of a chauvinistic disposition?" Justinian sighed out a draconic cloud of *Molto Sinistra* and took a languid guess, "Primeval pigs?"

"*Bachelors*[3]." Barnesworthe snapped the rifle into firing position, which brought the barrel up the forty-five degrees necessary to point ominously at Agent Justinian's nether regions. He drained his glass and concluded, as was often the case where Elaine Barnesworthe was concerned, that discretion was the better part of remaining attached to one's extremities.

Happily for both Ronald Justinian and his prospective progeny, the airship's first mate chose that precise moment to march through the door of their cabin and execute what he had intended to be a supremely masculine salute. Intentions being what they are, however (and Miss Barnesworthe's attire being what *it* was), he instead found himself executing a supremely piscine impression of a largemouth bass. The lady in question was decidedly unimpressed. "Don't bother to knock, then!" she barked as the gaping boy struggled to salvage some semblance of military decorum from the wreckage of his ingress. Justinian's quick gaze rapidly traced that of Lieutenant Carver as his partner twirled the slender firearm to rest deftly across her knees. "Oh, for God's sake, man—have you never seen a lady in trousers?" Reclined as he was on the lower berth, ankles crossed and libations in hand, the speed with which Just was across the floor and nose-to-nose with the lieutenant would have been unsettling under any circumstances, and Mr. Carver was considerably unsettled as it was.

"Heavens, sir, no! That is, not as such—that is, I wouldn't have thought—"

---

1 A moderately derogatory term for an "excessively" educated and intelligent female.

2 A highly derogatory term for persons of Italian or Spanish descent.

3 Intensely derogatory term for unmarried men. See "ponce" and "tosser."

"*Thought?* Take my advice, sir, and refrain from engaging in any such activity, as you are clearly unequal to the task!"

"Wha-? But, that is—how can? Awfully sor—I—" The lieutenant now appeared to be channeling the last moments of a choking basset hound.

"Damnation, sir! What do you want?" The sting of a direct demand seemed to jog Lt. Carver's memory; he wrenched himself to attention and returned smartly, "Beggin' your pardon, sir! The captain sends his compliments and requests that you and Miss Barnesworthe join him on the quarter-deck, sir!"

"Very good, then." Justinian extinguished his cigar in the dregs of the captain's best brandy and shoved the blackened concoction into Carver's unsteady hands. "Inform Captain Cook that Miss Barnesworthe and I shall join him presently. And be off with that, while you're at it." Carver scurried breathlessly from the cabin, clutching the snifter as if the entirety of his military future depended upon its safe delivery. Justinian stalked to the gilded mirror by the doorway and began the futile chore of unrumpling his perpetually rumpled suit, wrenching his knee-length coat about on his broad shoulders and jamming the silver buttons of his vest into a decent imitation of fashion and respectability. Barnesworthe's eyes were still twinkling mischievously from his performance with the lieutenant as she rose from the burgundy divan and slid into her own pea coat—a custom-fitted affair which settled effortlessly over her slight figure, outlining her every curve in brass and brown leather. Her thin fingers scampered over its absurd number of buttons and straps with practiced ease, and she soon had her rifle hung across her back on a length of braided hemp, a vision of professionalism and style.

Peering solicitously over Just's shoulders and tapping one toe of her knee-high Oxford leathers, she raised her eyebrows and blinked pointedly at the much-abused cravat her partner was presently twisting about his neck. "Lavender is not a masculine color, Just."

Justinian didn't take his eyes from his reflection. "Bully for lavender. This is violet."

Barnesworthe was not to be deterred. "The ability to distinguish between lavender and violet is not a masculine pursuit."

Justinian gave the cravat a final tug and rolled his head to stare wearily at his pugnacious partner. "Madam, you are on an airship whose crew has not seen shore leave for three months, and you are about to cross the deck wearing trousers which, incidentally, look as if they were painted on."

"Your point?"

"My point, *Signora* Barnesy, is that neither my masculinity nor my cravat will be commanding any serious attention on this voyage." Barnesworthe acquiesced with a nod. "*Touché*."

"*Merci*. Now, where are your gloves? It's not half cold out."

She slipped them on, savoring the smell of new leather as she appraised her own reflection. "Well, what would you expect? We are several hundred feet above the Channel in the dead of winter." Justinian shrugged into his grey wool overcoat with a grimace. "I would expect that someone would have concocted some plan of heating his bloody contraption. We're not Neanderthals—I mean, this is 19th century, dash it all." The tips of her gloved fingers rubbed distractedly together as Barnesworthe glanced sideways at her partner, her brows drawing imperceptibly closer together. "Are you really all that nervous, Just?"

"Heh? Nervous?

"Yes. You become excessively English under pressure."

Justinian snorted, an oddly feral sound. "Excessively English? I do nothing of the sort. Bosh, woman."

"'Bosh'? 'Dash it all'?" Barnesworthe cocked her head knowingly. "Really, old bean." Justinian ceased wrestling with his overcoat and sighed, one of his tanned hands instinctively stroking the aether-pistol at his belt like a trusted hound. He drew his eyes level with Barnesworthe's and spoke slowly, his voice dropping a weary octave. "You read the dispatch, Barnesy, same as me. You know what's waiting for us at Calais."

Barnesworthe turned to face him, her fingers now clenched together tight enough to make the new leather creak. "We can't be certain, Just. Communications have been down for a few days, but the French fleet might very well have—"

"The French, Barnesy? Truly? Do you really think so?" His voice was completely devoid of his customary sarcasm, which somehow made that desperate hope seem all the more mad. Elaine found her store of witty banter frighteningly bare in the silence that followed, filled only by the merciless hiss of wind across the porthole.

Agent Justinian lifted his sword cane from the umbrella stand with undue care and stood a moment, staring blankly through the comely union of silver and ebony. With another sharp sigh, Just shook himself like a bridled charger and turned to the door, offering his arm to Agent Barnesworthe in one of his many flourishes of Continental chivalry. "For queen and country, Miss Barnesworthe?" She took his arm with an easy smile. "For queen and country, Mr. Justinian."

~ ~ ~ ~ ~ ~ ~

Captain Gregory Cook was planted on the quarterdeck, one weathered hand on the tiller and the other twirling the dial of his Franklin goggles, the right lens telescoping over the port bow for a glimpse of the French shoreline. His mustache—solid silver and impeccably trimmed—twitched slightly, one of his more overt signs of irritation. "Jolly rotten business, this lot. Hm-mph. First Germany, six months ago, then Belgium, not two months after. And now France. Jolly rotten, I say. Eh, Carver?"

The lieutenant nodded and mumbled something vaguely affirmative. The captain was only including him in the conversation out of habit and good form, after all. That and the need to pretend he wasn't talking entirely to himself.

"Quite so, yes, hmm. And no news, either, Mr. Carver, none at all. Just a few telegrams sent off in a raging panic and then silence, every time. Nothing in, nothing out. Hm-mph. Most unusual."

The captain's telescopic survey stumbled over the form of Agent Barnesworthe as she emerged from beneath the forecastle, arm-in-arm with Agent Justinian, her lithe stride keeping remarkably good balance on the undulating deck of the *Batista*. Captain Cook whuffled sharply through his beard and snapped his Franklin lens shut, becoming suddenly intensely concerned with the rigging on the portside balloon.

"I say, Carver, do see to that lot up there. This is hardly the time to be losing altitude, after all. Hm-mph. No indeed. Off you go, then." The lieutenant slunk gratefully away as Justinian and Barnesworthe mounted the quarterdeck, with Just looking as if he would find breaking his cane over Carver's backside a most cathartic exercise indeed. The captain twirled off a salute with that particular flavor of dignity which only comes from thirty-two years of marinating in the Royal Air Force.

"Good morning, sir. Madam. I trust your passage thus far has been comfortable?" Justinian broke off scowling at Carver to return Cook's salute.

"Your accommodations have been admirable, Captain, thank you. Any word from Calais?" Captain Cook's face grew visibly longer, his graying hair rumpling in the morning breeze—Barnesworthe was struck by his sudden resemblance to a woeful and bedraggled walrus.

"Not a sound, sir. Hm-mph. Nary a peep, as they say. I don't need to explain to you two what this could mean for the Empire."

Justinian looked uncharacteristically grim. "No, captain. That will not be necessary."

Barnesworthe retrieved her arm from Justinian's and crossed quickly to the portside rail, leaning heavily on it and squinting through the mist. She called over her shoulder, "You are aware of our orders, then, Captain?" Cook straightened and set to twirling the dials of his goggles again, twitching his mustache and *harrumph*ing with distiction.

"Quite so, madam, hm-mph, of course! Yours is an operation of a clandestine nature, if I'm not mistaken."

"Yes, captain. Where do you intend to drop us?"

"Hm-mph, madam, that depends, I'm afraid. Hm, yes, indeed. You see, if all goes as planned, then a pair of aero-racers will be issued to you as soon as we are in sight of the Calais harbor. However, should we come under attack, as we very well may, hm-mph, our stratagem will require considerable, hmm, alteration." He blinked myopically from behind the goggles, one eye magnified comically. "Are you and Agent Justinian equipped to execute a, hmm, crash landing over the English Channel?"

Barnesworthe grinned darkly over her shoulder. "Is anyone?" Captain Cook whuffled appreciatively, clasping his hands behind his back with nautical flair and nodding smartly. "Quite so, madam. Hm-mph. Indeed. Must make do." The twinkle in his eye soon darkened as a squirrelly figure on the portside balloon caught his officious attention. He bellowed up at the first mate, "I say, Carver! What the devil do you think you're about? Keep tangling the rigging and we'll be swimming in a moment!" He stalked off, grumbling into his quivering mustache, "The man's been useless since breakfast. Hm-*mph.* You'd think he'd bloody well been bewitched—not *clockwise*, Carver! Have you taken leave of your senses?"

Justinian swaggered over to join Barnesworthe, practically whistling with vindictive glee. He leaned indolently on the rail, breathing deeply and surveying the horizon as if he were on holiday. Nonchalantly, he leaned slowly toward his partner and quietly asked, as if it were only a matter of passing fancy, "Do *you* know how to fly an aero-racer, Barnsey?"

Agent Barnesworthe blinked and pursed her lips. "*Tsk.* Of course I do. I was flying aero-racers before I could ride a horse."

"Ah." Agent Justinian nodded and continued to study the lightening sky with philosophical detachment. Barnesworthe narrowed her eyes. "Just…"

"Hmm?"

"You can't fly one, can you?" Justinian leaned his back against the railing and steepled his fingers thoughtfully.

"Well, that depends, really. Are they the ones shaped like a horseshoe, open in the front, with the rockets out to the side?"

"No, Just, they are not." Barnesworthe sounded as if she were explaining rudimentary maths to an inattentive boy in the second form. "You're thinking of an aethercar—aero-racers are the single-seated ones, rounded in the back and tapered in the front, like a leaf or spade."

"Ah." Justinian resumed his thoughtful silence, still nodding slowly, as if Barnesworthe had just given him a difficult bit of alchemy to decipher. His partner's eyes were narrowed to wrathful slits now, one gloved finger beginning to slowly tap the rail in mounting irritation. "Just," she patiently growled.

"Hmm?"

"Are you implying that we are about to attempt a covert landing—on foreign and possibly occupied soil, no less—in a vehicle which you have *neglected to learn how to operate?*"

Justinian folded his arms, glancing heavenward in dreamy resignation. "Well, you can't *really* expect me to keep up, can you? I mean, that Nikola Tevala comes out with a new aether-thingummy every fortnight, and I *am* a *profoundly* busy man…"

Barnesworthe was practically snarling now, baring her clenched teeth in frustration. "It's Nikola *Tesla*, you daft twit, and if you can't be bothered to keep your certification up to—"

"Land ho!"

Barnesworthe left off berating her nonplussed partner and dashed to the portside balloon in a streak of leather and gold. "Whereabouts, lieutenant?" Carver, still gainfully endeavoring to disentangle his knees from the rigging he'd mangled, waved his free arm toward the southeast, looking for all the world like a befuddled blue jay snarled in a fishing net. Barnesworthe resumed peering into the mist, sensing Justinian's sturdy form gliding to her side with practiced ease. The pair stood motionless for a moment.

"I don't know, Barnesy, I can't see a—"

"*Hands to quarters! Fighters off the starboard side!*" Captain Cook's English grumble had erupted into a martial roar, and the airship was instantly swarming with grey-coated airmen. Levers and cogs slid and spun wildly in a chaotic dance of military precision, aether-cannons emerging like brass genies from beneath the intricately paneled deck, and the two forward aetherguns whirling to starboard like a pair of Doberman Pinschers with their ears perked. Captain Cook continued to bellow at this crew: "Stand ready on the starboard side, there. Lieutenant Carver, if you are not at your post in less than twenty seconds, I will personally shoot you down myself, sir! *Move your Cockney hindquarters, man!*"

Agents Justinian and Barnesworthe were at the starboard side in a breath, a cannon between them as they stared through the fog, weapons at the ready. Justinian's sword cane was drawn, as was his trusty aether-pistol; he distantly realized that he couldn't actually remember drawing them. Barnesy calmly squinted through the long-distance sight on her rifle, slowing her breathing to the steady whisper of a veteran sniper. The bustle of the airmen around her faded to a dull hum as her world narrowed to the circle of roiling cloud in her sights.

The mist parted.

Her breath suddenly caught, tangled in her chest with her heartbeat. Her voice wriggled through the knot in her throat, a strangled gasp in the half-blink of absolute stillness before the explosion.

"What in God's name *are* they?"

Then the deck was ablaze, massive globs of electrified aether slamming into the wood and brass like fiery lather, frothing the *Batista* into a quivering, bleeding mass of green flames. There was a moment of stunned and concussive silence on the airship. Dazed and dizzy men stared blankly at burning or missing limbs, as if their minds had inexplicably lost the protocol to process this particular input. Then the screaming began in earnest. The second barrage hit before the first had finished burning, blasting the hydrogen in the starboard balloon into violent orange flame. Two or three airmen managed to fire their cannons, but their pitiful spurts had no more effect than would matches flung at a rabid bear.

Barnesworthe sleepily noticed that she was lying on something wooden and warm, an orange, ovoid sun shining remarkably close. She wondered vaguely who had let the sun get so close, and who had turned off all the sound, except for that tiresome ringing…

"Come along, Barnesy, time we were away."

The wooden warmth faded, and then strong, Italian hands were lifting her up, floating her away from the sun and the ringing. *Really*, she thought, *this will not do. What will mother say?* It was all very tiresome and dull, and she wished Albert was home from his ride. Wasn't it time for tea? It wasn't like him to be late, really. She was sitting comfortably now, hands primly folded, ankles properly crossed. Anyone could take her picture now, she was quite ready…

"Barnesy, come to! I can't fly this thing!"

What was that dreadful Italian on about? He oughtn't be in the garden, really, there were no peasants allowed in the garden. *Darling*, she murmured, *send the dreadful Italian away, I find him most tiresome*. Perhaps he is of the disadvantaged sort. Perhaps if we gave him some money, he would go away. Yes, that is the thing to do…

Justinian stooped over his half-conscious partner, feeling her pulse and fumbling his pockets for smelling salts, knowing full well he never carried such things. A third blast hit the ship, this time on the port side, listing the *Batista* over like a punch-drunk boxer and blasting the portside balloon into flames to match its partner. Justinian gasped and caught himself on the rising deck, the ship awash with green aether, orange flame, and bloodied men in assorted sizes and stages of dismemberment. He grudgingly hoped that Carver had managed to dismount the portside balloon before his untimely cremation. He kneeled before Agent Barnesworth, shaking her and shouting frantically, though he had quite forgotten whether it was Italian or English he was supposed to be speaking. Finally, in desperation, Just raised one hand and, holding his breath in terror, slapped Barnesworthe full in the face. She sat up shouting, "We are *not* amused!"

"Barnesy, darling!" Justinian kissed her fervently on both cheeks, losing himself in a relieved seizure of Latin elation. She slapped him off clumsily, batting her hands at him like an angry schoolgirl. "Oh, be off, you ridiculous man!" She stumbled to her feet, listing slightly and still waving away the attentions of her solicitous partner. "Now, how do things stand, Mr. Justinian?"

For some absurd reason, Just was grinning. Ridiculous man.

"Things do not stand, Miss Barnesworthe, I am afraid that they fall. And we will do the same if we're not aboard one of these infernal contraptions in a few moments." Agent Barnesworthe found herself being dizzily ushered into the tight cockpit of one of the *Batista*'s aero-racers, Just's untrained hands fumbling about with the straps in the driver's seat. She shoved him away, muttering, "Oh, be *off*, man, let me do it." She tied herself in in a moment and began flicking on the power coils by her knees, feeling the little engine purr itself cheerfully awake, sounding incongruously like a content housecat in an earthquake. Her hands were on the flight controls and poised for liftoff when she realized that Justinian was still standing beside her.

"What in God's name *are* you about, Just? Get in one and strap down, you'll pick it up in no time." Justinian didn't move. He was staring pensively over her head. He had an odd look on his face. Ridiculous man.

"It's not all that different from aethercar, I promise. And it's better than a burning airship." He still wasn't moving.

"Oh, for God's *sake*, Just! What are—"

"Barnesy."

Elaine Barnesworthe turned to follow her partner's gaze. They were at the far aft end of the *Batista*, in the holding bay for the airship's aeroracers. Elaine blinked slowly. There should have been dozens of the little crafts, all sitting in readiness, but instead there was simply a smoldering mass of green aether. The holding bay had been hit, and badly, probably by the first blast. It really was miraculous that even one aero-racer had survived. Barnesworthe turned and stared up at Just, who smiled glumly, "I'm due for a swim, then, aren't I?"

"No." She began struggling with the straps, scrabbling clumsily from the racer. "*No*, Just. I'm not going to—"

"Barnesy, go."

"Absolutely *not*, Just. Not without you. We'll find a way to fit us both in, and—"

"Don't be daft, woman, the thing's barely bigger than an oversized Shetland."

"Well, then *you* take it, Just, I'm not going—"

"*Agent Barnesworthe!*" He had her firmly by the shoulders and was glowering at her with wounded dignity. "We are on a sinking ship and this is the *only* lifeboat. Now, do you really think I intend to disembark while there is a lady onboard?"

Barnesworthe stood a moment, her gloved hands fumbling weakly and her vision going watery. Ridiculous *man*. Finally, she wrenched herself from his grasp and squirmed her way back into the aero-racer, muttering blearily, "Just as I said, most excessively *English*..."

Justinian steadied himself on the racer as a fourth barrage blasted the *Batista*, shouting over the roar of burning hydrogen, "Meet me in the Parc Richelieu at sundown two days from now, do you hear?" Barnesworthe nodded, tears beginning to stream freely down her face now. She turned to answer, but Justinian was dashing away down the burning deck. Muttering a stream of profanity to stifle her sobs, she lifted the aeroracer and began gliding slowly upwards.

Captain Gregory Cook was still stationed at the tiller with British doggedness, glaring forward like an irate wolfhound. Justinian bounded up, breathing heavily. "Going down with the ship then, captain?"

"No, sir! Waste of a good airship, that! I intend to crash her into their communications tower there." He pointed one gnarled hand at the approaching harbor, the tower in question blinking maliciously in the morning sun. Justinian's smile widened. "A blaze of glory it is, then."

"Only way to do it, Agent Justinian. *Hm-mph!* Only way, indeed. You will be disembarking presently, I presume?"

"Yes, sir! Allow me to offer my heartfelt thanks for the pleasant journey!" Cook's mustache curved upward, eyes twinkling again behind the smoky goggles, calling jovially after Justinian, "Be off, you rapscallion! And a pleasant landing to you!"

"And the same to you, sir!" Justinian caught sight of Barnesworthe's aero-racer as it slid past the starboard bow. He raced to the railing.

"*Elaine!*"

Agent Barnesworthe turned, and through her tears saw Ronald Justinian perched lightly on the rail of the *Batista*, grinning maniacally, one hand caught in the rigging, the smoke, wind, and flames whirling his overcoat about in manic splendor. He shouted through the storm:

"I wouldn't have missed it, Barnesy! I wouldn't have missed it for a knighthood!"

~ ~ ~ ~ ~ ~ ~

What awaits our beloved duo in Calais? Will Agent Justinian survive his aquatic plunge? Who is Jack Jeunes, and why this absurd affiliation for footnotes? Will there be danger? Will there be tears? More importantly, will there be tea!? The answers to all these and more can be found in the thrilling, titillating, and possibly tortuous upcoming chapter.

-Yours furtively, Jack Jeune.

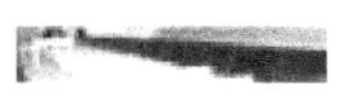

Reviews

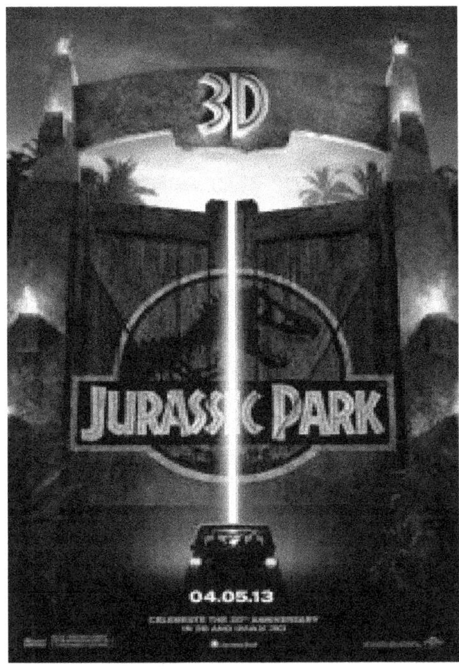

Jurassic Park 3D
1993, 127 min, Adventure | Sci-Fi
Director: Steven Spielberg
Writers: Michael Crichton (novel),
Michael Crichton (screenplay)
David Koepp (screenplay)
Stars: Sam Neill, Laura Dern, Jeff Goldblum

I was nine years old. My brother was six. We were both with my parents in Austin where my dad was attending a conference of some sort. I don't know if it was for his job as a high school football coach or if it was for his other job as the coordinator for the adult education program in our region. That's beside the point though. What matters is that one afternoon during the conference, my mom took my brother and me to see *Jurassic Park.*

The movie had been out for a few months by that point, and my parents, ever the avid movie-goers, had seen it shortly after it was released. Initially, given the reported amounts of terror in the film, my parents didn't think it was appropriate to take their toddlers along. After seeing the film though, my mom realized that *Jurassic Park* was more than your run-of-the-mill monster flick. *Jurassic Park* was cinematically significant. It was, and still is, a film that demanded to be seen in theaters on a field of vision engulfing screen surrounded by bone shaking speakers with as many other people as possible. Though it might terrify us, seeing *Jurassic Park* in a theater was, presumably, a unique life experience that my mother made sure my brother and I didn't miss.

Of course, my mom was wrong about one thing - 1993 wasn't the only chance we would have to see *Jurassic Park* in a theater. Life (or rather the market) found a way to give movie goers that opportunity once again. *Jurassic Park* has been re-released in theaters in IMAX 3D (and in regular 2D if you closely check your megaplex's showtime schedule) in "celebration" of its twentieth anniversary, though they really should have waited until June to launch the celebration. Releasing it now is a bit like having a birthday party two months before your birthday (Surprise!), though your birthday never has to compete with studios' summer tent-pole movies.

The real reason to go see *Jurassic Park* again isn't for the 3D. The film is already one of the most visually impressive of all time. The question of whether 3D conversion enhances *Jurassic Park* is best answered by that joke they tell about lingerie at bridal showers - it fits best when it's left on the floor.

The real reason to go see the movie again is for the big screen and especially for the big sound. The film feels frozen in time. It is a perfect mix of practical and digital special effects. No matter what John Hammond tells the lawyer, there are animatronics involved in Jurassic Park, unlike most big budget spectacle movies today which opt for only digital effects, and the careful mixture gives the movie it's teeth. My two favorite frightful moments in the film are animatronic. The first is when the t-rex comes through the sunroof of the jeep while trying to eat the children. The glass wasn't supposed to break, so the terror the kids show is real. The second is when we first see a velociraptor in the power shed. That's a "real" dinosaur head pushing aside the cables to pop out behind Dr. Sadler.

Jurassic Park both shows us something we've never seen before and makes us believe it's real. The movie perfects Hammond's flea circus illusion, and more than anything, that's the legacy of Jurassic Park. At Reel Spirituality, we spend a lot of time talking about story and theme and meaning, but often there is better theological ore to be mined in the filmmaking process than in the moral of the product. A film's place in movie history is sometimes more important than the content of the film itself.

Jurassic Park's morals - something about humanity's inablity to control life or humanity's need to "evolve" to care for others - are all well and good, but *Jurassic Park*'s method - showing audiences something impossible - proved far more compelling. The film is packed with shots of people being amazed at what they see. Spielberg is famous for his shots of faces caught in moments of visual wonder. *Jurassic Park* is wall to wall (fence to fence?) awe.

That's the part of *Jurassic Park* that got carried out into the world. While there had been earlier sparks (*Young Sherlock Holmes*, *Labyrinth*, *Terminator 2*), *Jurassic Park* set fire to the imaginations of filmmakers the world over. George Lucas, who oversaw post-production on Jurassic Park while Spielberg went to work on *Schindler's List*, realized technology would now enable him to make the *Star Wars* prequels he'd always wanted to make. Seeing *Jurassic Park* convinced Peter Jackson that his beloved *Lord of the Rings* books could finally be translated to the cinema.

Movies, because they have the ability to show us in seemingly real ways things we never dreamed possible, have the potential to inspire us to create new worlds. Sometimes those worlds involve dinosaurs. Other times they involve even more fantastic things like forgiveness, mercy, peacefulness, and compassion. Just as George Lucas and Peter Jackson took *Jurassic Park* seriously and created Naboo and Middle Earth, so we all can take it seriously and better respect life and care for others.

Twenty years ago, my mom took me to see *Jurassic Park* and showed me that movies matter. Twenty years later, I'm learning more and more why and how. She wanted me to see something remarkable, and I did. The more I watch, the more I see how very remarkable the movies can be.

—Elijah Davidson[1]

[1] Elijah Davidson's review of Jurassic Park 3D originally appeared on Reel Spirituality (http://www.brehmcenter.com/initiatives/reelspirituality/film/reviews/jurassic-park) and is reprinted here with permission from Reel Spirituality and the author.

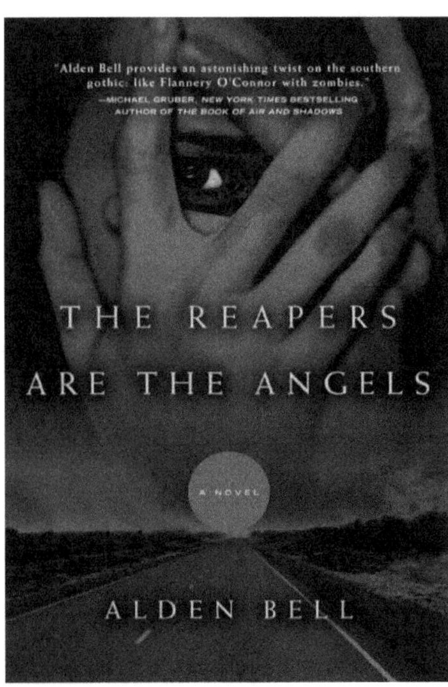

The Reapers Are the Angels
By Alden Bell
Henry Holt Publishers, 2010
225 PP.
Paperback $15.00

More Zombies? I was of the same opinion and have been for the last couple of years since the recent 'outbreak' of zombie related cultural artifacts—not that there haven't been very good and artistically, philosophically, socially, theologically thought-provoking incarnations of the zombie genre (there have been, as evidenced here by this novel); it's just that there have just been *so many* that the genre has been somewhat strained. So when I ran across this novel, and saw the back page tag line—"like Flannery O'Connor with zombies"—I was trepidatious. But I was pleasantly surprised when I found that the tagline resonated—this was a southern gothic or 'grotesque.' This novel is attempting, in some degree (and with some great success), that special 'unaccustomed realism' developed by Flannery O'Connor. As O'Connor noted, it is in

> …these grotesque works, we find that the writer has made alive some experience which we are not accustomed to observe every day, or which the ordinary man may never experience in his ordinary life. We find that connections which we would expect in the customary kind of realism have been ignored, that there are strange skips and gaps which anyone trying to describe manners and customs would certainly not have left. Yet the characters have an inner coherence, if not always a coherence to their social framework. Their fictional qualities lean away from typical social patterns, toward mystery and the unexpected.[1]

[1] Flannery O'Connor, *Mystery and Manners: Occasional Prose*, Ed. Sally and Robert Fitzgerald, New York: Farrar, Straus and Giroux, 1969, 40.

Joshua Gaylord (Alden Bell is his pseudonym) has built a detailed and well-rounded world where mystery and the unexpected coincide with rich characters (with an internal logic and coherence). From the first sentence of the novel we know we are not embarking on an ordinary zombie genre novel journey: "God is a slick God. Temple knows. She knows because of all the crackerjack miracles still to be seen on this ruined globe."[2] Our heroine, Temple, is a strong, smart and vulnerable character. As such, you are willingly pulled along into her story and her thoughts. It is refreshing to see full characterization as well—that fully realized characters inhabit this world. Something that Gaylord/Bell does so well is he never fully makes the zombies the central antagonists of the story. This allows for a deeper examination of the human condition. Also, as O'Connor might have it, he takes the ordinary and places it in a never-to-be-experienced-in-ordinary life situation—where customary connections can be unnoticed, where there are 'skips' and 'gaps,' where ordinary markers of manners and customs are seemingly gone. The central antagonist is Moses Todd, a menacing and intelligent character, who is, like Temple, aware of some deeper meaning to the goings on in the world. There is a sense (for both characters) of a quest and even of destiny—meaning *explicitly* comes in to play in this narrative. The characters and story raise the questions of meaning, as one would expect in the novelization of 'grotesque realism.' Without these questions of meaning (either explicitly or implicitly) a story can often become mechanized, instrumentalized—which can be a real danger especially in a zombie novel. With Moses Todd and Temple, the question of meaning is integral to the plot of the novel; it is explicitly part of the narrative, and not just something that happens meta-narratively. The narrative allows for the examination of the characters, and the readers themselves, as individuals and as a part of humanity, through these explicit questions of deeper meaning and mystery. The questions posed here are interwoven into the narrative. This focus on meaning within the actual narrative itself gives a sense of direction to those broad questions and avoids the ponderous and ambiguous nature of some other zombie genre cultural artifacts, which often attempt—and often fail at—(quasi) philosophical, intellectual relevance. Plus, this story is just a good yarn.

Gaylord/Bell has also written a sequel to *Reapers*, called *Exit Kingdom*, which apparently follows the character of Moses Todd. If his success in *Reapers* is carried over in any way in this new novel, it would be well worth the read.

—Jeff Sellars

---

[2] Alden Bell, *The Reapers Are the Angels*, New York: Henry Holt and Company, LLC, 2010, 3.

Notes on Contributors

Jake Andrews is currently a post-doctoral research associate in the Cambridge Inter-faith Programme. His research interests include Augustinian theology, theological hermeneutics, and intersections of art and theology. He will assume a place in the MFA program at the Iowa Writers' Workshop in August 2013.

Mark J. Boone has a B. A. in Biblical Studies and Philosophy from Dallas Baptist University (2005) and a Ph.D. in Philosophy from Baylor University (2010). He has taught at Berry College in Rome, GA, for two years and is currently an Assistant Professor of Philosophy at Forman Christian College in Lahore, Pakistan. His specializations are in the history of philosophy, especially ancient and medieval philosophy.

Elijah Davidson is Co-Director of Reel Spirituality, an initiative of faith and film at Brehm Center for Worship, Theology, and the Arts at Fuller Seminary. He reviews films currently in theaters weekly for Reel Spirituality's website as well as hosting Reel Spirituality's bi-weekly podcast, and he is the managing editor for all content published on Brehm Center's website. He and his wife, Krista, live in Imperial Beach, California.

Daniel J. Heisey, O. S. B., is a Benedictine monk of Saint Vincent Archabbey, Latrobe, Pennsylvania, where he is known as Brother Bruno. A graduate of the University of Cambridge, he teaches Church History at Saint Vincent Seminary.

Kevin C. Neece is a writer and speaker in Fort Worth, Texas. He is a media and pop culture columnist for *New Identity Magazine* and blogger for Art House Dallas whose work has appeared in *Rethinking Everything Magazine, Next Wave Magazine*, *Worldview Church Report* and *Baptist Life*, among others. He is also a contributing editor for *Imaginatio et Ratio: A Journal of Theology and the Arts*. Kevin holds a BAS in Communication and Philosophy and an MLA in Fine Arts. He has taught university courses on fine arts, critical thinking and cultural engagement and has lectured frequently on media, the arts and pop culture from a Christian worldview perspective. Kevin's current work includes The Undiscovered Country Project--an ongoing journey through *Star Trek* from a Christian worldview perspective--and Jesus Films 101, an exploration of Christ in cinema that draws on his 20 years of research in the field.

Caitlin Smith is currently working on her Master's degree in English at the University of Texas, Arlington and hopes to return to Dallas Baptist University, where she received her B.A. in Communications, as a teacher. She is locally known as The Fairy Girl, for all her research deals with fairy tales and fantasy, and she can be spotted dancing around Scarborough Faire with wings and pointed ears. Caitlin loves to write, and she has won a few contests, but this is her first published piece.

Jaclyn Young is a graduate of Dallas Baptist University. She wrote her Bachelor's Thesis on the history, ideology, and expressions of the Steampunk Movement. She is presently working as a writer in South Asia. She blogs at http://glitterlessgold.blogspot.com.

www.ingramcontent.com/pod-product-compliance
Lightning Source LLC
LaVergne TN
LVHW061255100826
845148LV00008B/1128
9781625644305